2-14

D1556217

25 Complex Text Passages to Meet the Common Core

Literature and Informational Texts

Grade 6

by Martin Lee and Marcia Miller

NEW YORK ● TORONTO ● LONDON ● AUCKLAND ● SYDNEY
MEXICO CITY ● NEW DELHI ● HONG KONG ● BUENOS AIRES

Teaching *Resources*

Cover design: Scott Davis
Interior design: Kathy Massaro

Interior illustrations: Delana Bettoli and Kate Flanagan © 2014 by Scholastic Inc.

Image credits: page 30 © jgareri/iStockphoto; page 34 © Josemaria Toscano/Shutterstock, Inc.;
page 36 © SongSpeckels/iStockphoto; page 38 © nature78/Big Stock Photo; page 44 © Pinkerton; page 46 © Joanne Ryder;
page 48 © spline_x/Shutterstock, Inc.; page 56 © Mark Herreid/Shutterstock, Inc.; page 58 (top) © Terence Mendoza/Shutterstock,
Inc.; page 58 (bottom) © Dja65/Shutterstock, Inc; page 60 © Library and Archives of Canada; page 62 © NASA;
page 66 © ALMA (ESO/NAOJ/NRAO); page 68 © Superstock, Inc.; page 74 © Shawn Zhang/Shutterstock, Inc.

ISBN: 978-0-545-57712-0
Copyright © 2014 by Scholastic Inc.
All rights reserved.
Printed in the U.S.A.
Published by Scholastic Inc.

1 2 3 4 5 6 7 8 9 10   40   21 20 19 18 17 16 15 14

Contents

Introduction 4

Connections to the Common Core State Standards 12

Teaching Notes 13

Literature Passages

1. **Gym Jam** • Realistic Fiction 26

2. **The Golden Axe** • Fable 28

3. **Sounds of Spring** • Humorous Monologue 30

4. **What Goes Around...** • Folktale 32

5. **City in the Sky** • Travel Fiction 34

6. **Thief of Fire** • Myth 36

7. **Out Back of Beyond** • Magical Realism 38

8. **Dogs and a Dinghy** • Problem-Solution Story 40

9. **Ship's Boy** • Historical Fiction 42

Informational Text Passages

10. **Private Eye** • Word Origin Article 44

11. **A Writer's Story** • Author Interview 46

12. **Ancient Survivor** • Botany Essay 48

13. **Lessons From Superheroes** • Popular Culture Essay 50

14. **Impossible Not to Smile** • Biographical Sketch 52

15. **Ellis Island of the West** • History Essay 54

16. **Game of Change** • Sports History Essay 56

17. **Preserving Audio Archives** • Speech 58

18. **The Sky's the Limit** • Architecture/History Essay 60

19. **Not Rocket Science** • Science/History Essay 62

20. **Surprises in Ice** • Environmental Science Article/Graph ... 64

21. **Astronomers' Desert** • Geography/Science Article 66

22. **The Great Wall of Los Angeles** • Art Essay 68

23. **Bad Burger** • e-mail Business Letter 70

24. **Off-Leash** • Letter to the Editor 72

25. **Table Tennis** • Technical Writing/Game Guide 74

Answers 76

"To build a foundation for college and career readiness, students must read widely and deeply from among a broad range of high-quality, increasingly challenging literary and informational texts. Through extensive reading of stories, dramas, poems, and myths from diverse cultures and different time periods, students gain literary and cultural knowledge as well as familiarity with various text structures and elements. By reading texts in history/social studies, science, and other disciplines, students build a foundation of knowledge in these fields that will also give them the background to be better readers in all content areas. Students can only gain this foundation when the curriculum is intentionally and coherently structured to develop rich content knowledge within and across grades. Students also acquire the habits of reading independently and closely, which are essential to their future success."

—COMMON CORE STATE STANDARDS FOR ENGLISH LANGUAGE ARTS, JUNE 2010

25 Complex Text Passages to Meet the Common Core: Literature and Informational Texts —Grade 6 includes complex reading passages with companion comprehension question pages for teaching the two types of texts—Literature and Informational—covered in the Common Core State Standards (CCSS) for English Language Arts. The passages and lessons in this book address the rigorous expectations put forth by the CCSS "that students read increasingly complex texts through the grades." This book embraces nine of the ten CCSS College and Career Readiness Anchor Standards for Reading that inform solid instruction for literary and informational texts.

Anchor Standards for Reading

Key Ideas and Details

1. Read closely to determine what the text says explicitly and make logical inferences from it; cite specific textual evidence when writing or speaking to support conclusions drawn from the text.

2. Determine central ideas or themes of a text; summarize key supporting details and ideas.

3. Analyze how and why individuals, events, and ideas develop and interact throughout a text.

Craft and Structure

4. Interpret words and phrases as they are used in a text, including determining technical, connotative, and figurative meanings, and analyze how specific word choices shape meaning or tone.

5. Analyze the structure of texts, including how specific sentences, paragraphs, and larger portions of text relate to each other and the whole.

6. Assess how point of view or purpose shapes the content and style of a text.

Integration of Knowledge and Ideas

7. Integrate and evaluate content presented in diverse media and formats, including visually and quantitatively, as well as in words.

8. Delineate and evaluate the argument and specific claims in a text, including the validity of the reasoning as well as the relevance and sufficiency of the evidence.

Range of Reading and Level of Text Complexity

10. Read and comprehend complex literary and informational texts independently and proficiently.

The materials in this book also address the Language Standards, including skills in the conventions of standard English, knowledge of language, and vocabulary acquisition and use. In addition, students meet Writing Standards as they answer questions about the passages, demonstrating their ability to convey ideas coherently, clearly, and with support from the text. On page 12, you'll find a correlation chart that details how the 25 passages meet specific standards. This information can also be found with the teaching notes for each passage on pages 13–25.

About Text Complexity

The CCSS recommend that students tackle increasingly complex texts to develop and hone their skills and knowledge. Many factors contribute to the complexity of any text.

Text complexity is more intricate than a readability score alone reveals. Most formulas examine sentence length and structure and the number of difficult words. Each formula gives different weight to different factors. Other aspects of text complexity include coherence, organization, motivation, and any prior knowledge readers may bring.

A complex text can be relatively easy to decode, but if it examines complex issues or uses figurative language, the overall text complexity rises. By contrast, a text that uses unfamiliar words may be less daunting if readers can apply word-study skills and context clues effectively to determine meaning.

This triangular model used by the CCSS shows three distinct yet interrelated factors that contribute to text complexity.

CCSS Model of Text Complexity

Qualitative measures consider the complexity of meaning or purpose, structure, language conventionality, and overall clarity.

Quantitative measures complexity in terms of word length and frequency, sentence length, and text cohesion. Lexile® algorithms rank this type of complexity on a numerical scale.

Reader and Task considerations refer to such variables as a student's motivation, knowledge, and experience brought to the text, and the purpose, complexity, and types of questions posed.

About the Passages

The 25 reproducible, one-page passages included in this book are divided into two categories. The first 9 passages represent literature (fiction) and are followed by 16 informational texts (nonfiction). Each grouping presents a variety of genres and forms, organizational structures, purposes, tones, and tasks. Consult the table of contents (page 3) to see the scope of genres, forms, and types of content-area texts. The passages within each category are arranged in order of Lexile score (the quantitative measure), from lowest to highest, and fall within the Lexile score ranges recommended for sixth graders. The Lexile scores for grade 6, revised to reflect the more rigorous demands of the CCSS, range from 925 to 1070. For more about determinations of complexity levels, see page 5 and pages 8–9.

Each passage appears on its own page beginning with the title, the genre or form of the passage, and an opening question to give students a focus to keep in mind as they read. Some passages also include visual elements, such as photographs, drawings, illustrations, or tables, as well as typical text elements, such as italics, boldface type, bulleted or numbered lists, subheadings, or sidebars.

The line numbers that appear to the left of each passage will help you and your students readily locate a specific line of text. For example, students might say, "I'm not sure how to pronounce the name here in line 30." They might also include line numbers to identify text evidence when they answer questions about the piece. For example: "The author says in lines 11–13 that…"

The passages are stand-alone texts, and can be used in any order you choose. Feel free to assign passages to individuals, small groups, or the entire class, as best suits your teaching style. However, it's a good idea to preview each passage before you assign it, to ensure that your students have the skills needed to complete it successfully. (See page 10 for a close-reading routine to model for students.)

About the After-Reading Question Pages

The Common Core standards suggest that assessment should involve "text-dependent questions." Questions constructed to meet this demand guide students to cite evidence from the text. They fall into three broad categories: 1) Key Ideas and Details, 2) Craft and Structure, and 3) Integration of Knowledge and Ideas. According to the standards, responses should include claims supported by the text, connections to informational or literary elements found within the text explicitly or by logical implication, and age-appropriate analyses of themes or topics.

Following each passage is a reproducible page with six text-dependent comprehension questions for students to answer after reading. Two are multiple-choice questions that call for a single response and a brief text-based explanation to justify that choice. The other questions are open response items. These address a range of comprehension strategies and skills. Students can revisit the passage to find the evidence they need to answer each question. All questions share the goal of ensuring that students engage in close reading of the text, grasp its key ideas, and provide text-based evidence in their answers. In addition, the questions are formatted to reflect the types of questions that will be asked on standardized tests. The questions generally proceed from easier to more complex:

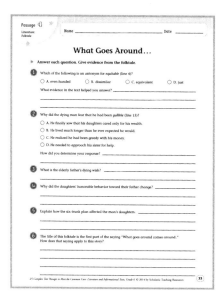

❋ The **least challenging** questions call for basic understanding and recall of details. They involve referencing the text verbatim or paraphrasing it. This kind of question might also ask students to identify a supporting detail an author did or did not include when making a persuasive argument.

❋ The **mid-level** questions call upon students to use mental processes beyond basic recall. To answer these questions, students may need to use context clues to unlock the meaning of unfamiliar words and phrases (including figurative language), classify or compare information, make inferences, distinguish facts from opinions, or make predictions. Such a question might also ask students to summarize the main idea(s) of a passage.

❋ The **deeper** questions focus on understanding that goes beyond the text. Students may need to recognize the author's tone and purpose, make inferences about the entire passage, or use logic to make predictions. This kind of question might even call upon students to determine why an author began or ended the passage as he or she did.

You may find it useful to have students reference line numbers from the passage for efficiency and clarity when they formulate answers. They can also refer to the line numbers during class discussions. Provide additional paper so students have ample space to write complete and thorough answers.

An answer key (pages 76–80) includes sample answers based on textual evidence and specific line numbers from the passage that support the answers. You might want to review answers with the whole class. This approach provides opportunities for discussion, comparison, extension, reinforcement, and correlation to other skills and lessons in your current plans. Your observations can direct the kinds of review and reinforcement you may want to add to subsequent lessons.

About the Teaching Notes

Each passage in this book is supported by a set of teaching notes found on pages 13–25.

In the left column, you will see the following features for each set of teaching notes.

❋ Grouping (**Literature** or **Informational Text**) and the genre or form of the piece.

❋ **Focus** statement describing the essential purpose of the passage, its main features, areas of emphasis, and what students will gain by reading it.

❋ **Teaching Tips** to help you motivate, support, and guide students before, during, and after reading. These easy-to-use suggestions are by no means exhaustive, and you may choose to add or substitute your own ideas or strategies.

- **Before Reading** tips include ways to introduce a passage, explain a genre, present a topic, discuss a format, introduce key vocabulary, or put a theme in context. A tip may suggest how to engage prior knowledge, connect with similar materials in other curriculum areas, or build motivation.

- **During Reading** tips offer possible procedures to help students work through the text, ideas for highlighting key words or concepts, suggestions for graphic organizers, and so on.

- **After Reading** tips provide follow-up questions, discussion topics, extension activities, further readings, or writing assignments linked to the text.

In the right column, are the essential CCSS connections for the passage sorted according to the specific sections of the document: **RL** (Reading Standards for Literature) or **RI** (Reading Standards for Informational Text), **W** (Writing Standards), and **L** (Language Standards). The CCSS chart on page 12 provides the correlations for the entire book at a glance and a URL for the CCSS website where you can find the specific wording of each skill.

Under the essential CCSS connections, you will find a **Complexity Index**, which offers analytical information about the passage based on the three aspects of text complexity, briefly summarized on the next page.

* **Quantitative** value, represented by a Lexile score.

* **Qualitative** rating, which appears in a matrix that presents four aspects of this measure:

  * **Meaning** for literary texts (single level of meaning ↔ multiple levels of meaning) or **Purpose** for informational texts (explicitly stated purpose ↔ implicit purpose)

  * **Structure** (simple ↔ complex organization; simple ↔ complex graphics)

  * **Language** (literal ↔ figurative; clear ↔ ambiguous; familiar ↔ unusual; conversational ↔ formal)

  * **Knowledge** (life experience; content expectations; cultural or literary background needed)

Each of the above aspects are ranked from 1 to 5, briefly summarized, as follows:

1	2	3	4	5
Simple, clear text; accessible language, ideas, and/or structure	Mostly linear with explicit meaning/purpose; clear structure; moderate vocabulary; assumes some knowledge	May have more than one meaning/purpose; some figurative language; more demanding structure, syntax, language, and/or vocabulary; assumes some knowledge	Multiple meanings/purposes possible; more sophisticated syntax, structure, language, and/or vocabulary; assumes much knowledge	May require inference and/or synthesis; complex structure, syntax, language, and/or vocabulary; assumes extensive knowledge

* **Reader and Task** considerations comprise two or more bulleted points. Ideas relating to the reader appear first, followed by specific suggestions for a text-based task. Reader and Task considerations also appear embedded within the teaching notes as well as in the guiding question that opens each passage and in the comprehension questions. Keep in mind that Reader and Task considerations are the most variable of the three measures of text complexity. Reader issues relate to such broad concerns as prior knowledge and experience, cognitive abilities, reading skills, motivation by and engagement with the text, and content and/or theme concerns. Tasks are typically questions to answer, ideas to discuss, or activities to help students navigate and analyze the text, understand key ideas, and deepen comprehension. The same task may be stimulating for some students but daunting to others. Because you know your students best, use your judgment to adjust and revise tasks as appropriate.

Teaching Routine to Support Close Reading

Complex texts become more accessible to readers who are able to use various strategies during the reading process. One of the best ways to scaffold students through this process is to model a close-reading routine.

* **Preview the text.** Help students learn to identify clues about the meaning, purpose, or goal of the text. They can first read the title and the guiding question that precedes the passage. In literary texts, students can scan for characters' names and clues about setting and time frame. In informational texts, students can use features such as paragraph subheadings and supporting photos, illustrations, or other graphics to get a sense of the organization and purpose.

* **Quick-read to get the gist.** Have students do a "run-through" individual reading of the passage to get a sense of it. The quick-read technique can also help students identify areas of confusion or problem vocabulary. You can liken this step to scanning a new store to get a sense of how it is set up, what products it sells, and how you can find what you need.

* **Read closely.** Next, have students read the same piece again, this time with an eye to unlocking its deeper meaning or purpose. For most students, this is the time to use sticky notes, highlighter pens, margin notes, or graphic organizers to help them work their way through the important parts of the text. You might provide text-related graphic organizers, such as T-charts, compare/contrast and Venn diagrams, character and concept maps, cause-and-effect charts, or evidence/conclusion tables.

* **Respond to the text.** Now it's time for students to pull their ideas together and for you to assess their understanding. This may involve summarizing, reading aloud, holding group discussions, debates, or answering written questions. When you assign the after-reading question pages, suggest that students reread questions as needed before they attempt an answer. Encourage them to return to the text as well. Remind students to provide text-based evidence as part of every answer. Finally, consider with students the big ideas of a piece, its message, lesson, or purpose, and think about how to extend learning.

Above all, use the passages and teaching materials in this book to inspire students to become mindful readers—readers who delve deeply into a text to get the most out of it. Help your students recognize that reading is much more than just decoding all the words. Guide them to dig in, think about ideas, determine meaning, and grasp messages.

The following page presents three copies of a reproducible, six-step guide to mindful reading. It is intended as a reusable prompt. Students can keep it at hand to help them recall, apply, and internalize close-reading strategies whenever they read.

How to Be
A Mindful Reader

Preview the text.
- Set a purpose for reading.

Read carefully.
- Slow down and stay focused.
- Monitor your understanding.

Read again.
- You might notice new information.

Take notes.
- Mark difficult words or phrases.
- Write questions in the margin.
- Make connections between ideas.

Summarize.
- Add headings.
- Jot down the main ideas.
- List the events in sequence.

Think about it.
- Read between the lines. What's the message?
- Do you agree or disagree?
- Has anything been left out?

How to Be
A Mindful Reader

Preview the text.
- Set a purpose for reading.

Read carefully.
- Slow down and stay focused.
- Monitor your understanding.

Read again.
- You might notice new information.

Take notes.
- Mark difficult words or phrases.
- Write questions in the margin.
- Make connections between ideas.

Summarize.
- Add headings.
- Jot down the main ideas.
- List the events in sequence.

Think about it.
- Read between the lines. What's the message?
- Do you agree or disagree?
- Has anything been left out?

How to Be
A Mindful Reader

Preview the text.
- Set a purpose for reading.

Read carefully.
- Slow down and stay focused.
- Monitor your understanding.

Read again.
- You might notice new information.

Take notes.
- Mark difficult words or phrases.
- Write questions in the margin.
- Make connections between ideas.

Summarize.
- Add headings.
- Jot down the main ideas.
- List the events in sequence.

Think about it.
- Read between the lines. What's the message?
- Do you agree or disagree?
- Has anything been left out?

Connections to the Common Core State Standards

As shown in the chart below, the teaching resources in this book will help you meet many of the reading, writing, and language standards for grade 6 outlined in the CCSS. For details on these standards, visit the CCSS website: www.corestandards.org/the-standards/.

Passage	Reading: Literature							Reading: Informational Text									Writing		Language					
	RL.6.1	RL.6.2	RL.6.3	RL.6.4	RL.6.5	RL.6.6	RL.6.10	RI.6.1	RI.6.2	RI.6.3	RI.6.4	RI.6.5	RI.6.6	RI.6.7	RI.6.8	RI.6.10	W.6.9	W.6.10	L.6.1	L.6.2	L.6.3	L.6.4	L.6.5	L.6.6
1	•	•	•	•	•	•	•										•	•	•	•	•	•	•	•
2	•	•	•	•	•	•	•										•	•	•	•	•	•	•	•
3	•	•	•	•	•	•	•										•	•	•	•	•	•	•	•
4	•	•	•	•	•	•	•										•	•	•	•	•	•	•	•
5	•	•	•	•	•	•	•										•	•	•	•	•	•	•	•
6	•	•	•	•	•	•	•										•	•	•	•	•	•	•	•
7	•	•	•	•	•	•	•										•	•	•	•	•	•	•	•
8	•	•	•	•	•	•	•										•	•	•	•	•	•	•	•
9	•	•	•	•	•	•	•										•	•	•	•	•	•	•	•
10								•	•	•	•	•	•	•		•	•	•	•	•	•	•	•	•
11								•	•	•	•	•	•	•		•	•	•	•	•	•	•	•	•
12								•	•	•	•	•	•	•	•	•	•	•	•	•	•	•	•	•
13								•	•	•	•	•	•		•	•	•	•	•	•	•	•	•	•
14								•	•	•	•	•	•		•	•	•	•	•	•	•	•	•	•
15								•	•	•	•	•	•	•		•	•	•	•	•	•	•	•	•
16								•	•	•	•	•	•	•		•	•	•	•	•	•	•	•	•
17								•	•	•	•	•	•	•	•	•	•	•	•	•	•	•	•	•
18								•	•	•	•	•	•	•		•	•	•	•	•	•	•	•	•
19								•	•	•	•	•	•		•	•	•	•	•	•	•	•	•	•
20								•	•	•	•	•	•	•		•	•	•	•	•	•	•	•	•
21								•	•	•	•	•	•	•	•	•	•	•	•	•	•	•	•	•
22								•	•	•	•	•	•	•		•	•	•	•	•	•	•	•	•
23								•	•	•	•	•	•		•	•	•	•	•	•	•	•	•	•
24								•	•	•	•	•	•		•	•	•	•	•	•	•	•	•	•
25								•	•	•	•	•	•	•		•	•	•	•	•	•	•	•	•

Passage 1   Gym Jam • page 26

Literature: Realistic Fiction

▶ **Focus** In this story, students explore character and setting as they read about a common problem and its realistic resolution.

▶ **Teaching Tips**

Before Reading
* Invite students to share prior experiences they have had as newcomers in a school, group, or community. List common concerns, questions, and adjustment strategies.

During Reading
* Guide readers to jot down comments about Mikayla's character and attitudes in the margins as they read.

After Reading
* Have students write a summary of Mikayla that includes her current situation and personality traits. Challenge them to predict possible outcomes for her beyond the story.

Common Core Connections

RL.6.1, RL.6.2, RL.6.3, RL.6.4, RL.6.5, RL.6.6, RL.6.10 • W.6.9, W.6.10 • L.6.1, L.6.2, L.6.3, L.6.4, L.6.5, L.6.6

Complexity Index

Quantitative: Lexile 930

Qualitative	1	2	3	4	5
Meaning	❋				
Structure	❋				
Language	❋				
Knowledge	❋				

Reader & Task

* The issues faced by a new student in school will be familiar and motivating to most readers.
* Encourage students to focus on the changes in Mikayla as the piece progresses.

Passage 2   The Golden Axe • page 28

Literature: Fable

▶ **Focus** This descriptive retelling of an Aesop fable challenges readers to understand the actions of its characters to interpret its moral lesson.

▶ **Teaching Tips**

Before Reading
* Engage prior knowledge of fables from Aesop and other cultural traditions.

During Reading
* Tell students to highlight unfamiliar words, phrases, or ideas for later discussion.

After Reading
* Have students summarize the story in their own words.
* Challenge students to write a character sketch of the humble woodcutter as a follow-up to answering question 5 (page 29).

Common Core Connections

RL.6.1, RL.6.2, RL.6.3, RL.6.4, RL.6.5, RL.6.6, RL.6.10 • W.6.9, W.6.10 • L.6.1, L.6.2, L.6.3, L.6.4, L.6.5, L.6.6

Complexity Index

Quantitative: Lexile 940

Qualitative	1	2	3	4	5
Meaning		❋			
Structure	❋				
Language		❋			
Knowledge		❋			

Reader & Task

* Most students will be familiar with the characteristics of a fable and its concluding lesson or moral.
* Encourage students to look for similarities and differences between the main character and the other woodcutters who learn of his story. Also have them notice Mercury's responses.

Literature: Humorous Monologue

▶ **Focus** This humorous monologue gives students the opportunity to explore point of view and elements of humor, such as exaggeration, understatement, imaginative idioms, and surprise.

▶ **Teaching Tips**

Before Reading
- Discuss the concept of *personification* in literature and in visual media.

During Reading
- Form reading groups with at least one member who is knowledgeable about baseball and familiar with some of its colorful language and expressions.
- Encourage readers to highlight vivid verbs and descriptive adjectives, and also circle expressions they need to have clarified.

After Reading
- Direct students to online resources they can use to verify the meanings of baseball expressions that appear in this piece.

Common Core Connections

RL.6.1, RL.6.2, RL.6.3, RL.6.4, RL.6.5, RL.6.6, RL.6.10 • W.6.9, W.6.10 • L.6.1, L.6.2, L.6.3, L.6.4, L.6.5, L.6.6

Complexity Index

Quantitative: Lexile 950

Qualitative	1	2	3	4	5
Meaning		✳			
Structure		✳			
Language				✳	
Knowledge				✳	

Reader & Task

- This passage will be of high interest to sports enthusiasts. However, students who have little knowledge of baseball may find the jargon in this piece challenging.
- Have readers share their responses to question 6 (page 31) to describe the various techniques the author uses to add humor to this monologue.

Literature: Folktale

▶ **Focus** This passage challenges readers to use inference to understand characters' motivations and detect deeper messages in a cautionary folktale from the Hindu tradition.

▶ **Teaching Tips**

Before Reading
- Preview challenging vocabulary in this tale, such as *substantial, fraught, isolation, cold-heartedness, ingrates, robust, rupees, solemn, amplified,* and *demise.*

During Reading
- Guide readers to summarize the main idea of each paragraph to ensure understanding.
- Encourage students to read between the lines to explain how actions and events in the story affect its characters.

After Reading
- Have students write a brief summary of this tale, explaining how characters' attitudes and emotions drove their actions.

Common Core Connections

RL.6.1, RL.6.2, RL.6.3, RL.6.4, RL.6.5, RL.6.6, RL.6.10 • W.6.9, W.6.10 • L.6.1, L.6.2, L.6.3, L.6.4, L.6.5, L.6.6

Complexity Index

Quantitative: Lexile 970

Qualitative	1	2	3	4	5
Meaning				✳	
Structure		✳			
Language				✳	
Knowledge			✳		

Reader & Task

- Students may need help drawing inferences and thinking critically to grasp the message of this folktale.
- Provide a graphic organizer students can use to diagram the plot, indicating the problem and resolution, and another one for analyzing the characters' motivations and behaviors.

Literature: Travel Fiction

▶ **Focus** This example of travel writing uses descriptive language, precise nouns, vivid verbs, site-specific facts, and personal reflections to help students visualize a unique setting.

▶ **Teaching Tips**

Before Reading
• Discuss the purpose and nature of travel writing.
• Preview specific geographic and historical terms related to indigenous life in the American Southwest: *mesa, pueblo, adobe, sandstone, conquistadors,* and *mission.* Model how to pronounce Acoma (AK-uh-muh).

During Reading
• Encourage students to consult a dictionary for challenging words whose meanings they cannot fully discern from context.
• Help students distinguish between facts and the writer's personal responses to them.

After Reading
• Have students write questions they would ask Leroy the tour guide, Leroy's father, the mission's caretaker, or the writer of the piece. Extend by having students research answers to their questions using online resources about the Acoma Pueblo.

Common Core Connections

RL.6.1, RL.6.2, RL.6.3, RL.6.4, RL.6.5, RL.6.6, RL.6.10 • W.6.9, W.6.10 • L.6.1, L.6.2, L.6.3, L.6.4, L.6.5, L.6.6

Complexity Index

Quantitative:
Lexile 1000

Qualitative	1	2	3	4	5
Meaning		*			
Structure		*			
Language				*	
Knowledge				*	

Reader & Task

• Students may be unfamiliar with the landscape and history of the New Mexico area.
• Tell students to look for characteristics and features of travel writing.

Literature: Myth

▶ **Focus** This classical Greek myth of defiance and retribution offers students an opportunity to explore character and cause-and-effect in a colorful retelling.

▶ **Teaching Tips**

Before Reading
• Brainstorm names and places students know from Greek mythology.
• Model how to pronounce *Zeus* [züs] and *Prometheus* [pruh-ME-thee-us].

During Reading
• As they read, have students jot down character traits of Zeus and Prometheus.
• Guide readers to notice details in the illustration that support the text.

After Reading
• Invite students to read another version of the Prometheus story, and then compare and contrast the two selections. Extend by having them read about Pandora and how Zeus used her to punish mortals.

Common Core Connections

RL.6.1, RL.6.2, RL.6.3, RL.6.4, RL.6.5, RL.6.6, RL.6.10 • W.6.9, W.6.10 • L.6.1, L.6.2, L.6.3, L.6.4, L.6.5, L.6.6

Complexity Index

Quantitative:
Lexile 1010

Qualitative	1	2	3	4	5
Meaning			*		
Structure		*			
Language				*	
Knowledge				*	

Reader & Task

• Some students may be unfamiliar with Greek mythology or with myths in general.
• Have students describe the differences in character between Zeus and Prometheus.

Literature: Magical Realism

▶ **Focus** This example of magical realism offers students an opportunity to identify foreshadowing clues that help predict what may happen.

▶ **Teaching Tips**

Before Reading

- Discuss the genre of magical realism. Explain that it is a type of fiction in which magical or fantastical events occur in a narrative that otherwise seems realistic.
- Review the characteristics of legendary monsters, for example, the Yeti (Abominable Snowman) and Loch Ness monster. Students may be familiar with Sasquatch by its other name, Big Foot.
- Present the words *omen* and *ominous*. Discuss their meaning and relationship.

During Reading

- Guide readers to highlight words or phrases in the text that foreshadow things to come, for example, the phrase *little-used trail*.
- Invite pairs to read the story aloud dramatically, alternating paragraphs.

After Reading

- Instruct students to revisit the text and identify details that seem magical or fantastic and those that seem realistic.
- Extend by having students write additional dialogue for the story or to retell the legend from Sasquatch's point of view.

Common Core Connections

RL.6.1, RL.6.2, RL.6.3, RL.6.4, RL.6.5, RL.6.6, RL.6.10 • W.6.9, W.6.10 • L.6.1, L.6.2, L.6.3, L.6.4, L.6.5, L.6.6

Complexity Index

Quantitative: Lexile 1040

Qualitative	1	2	3	4	5
Meaning		✳			
Structure			✳		
Language			✳		
Knowledge			✳		

Reader & Task

- Some students may be acquainted with tales of human interaction with outlandish creatures.
- Have students in small groups share and discuss the foreshadowing clues they found and how those clues may have helped them predict what would happen.

Passage 8 **Dogs and a Dinghy** • page 40

Literature: Problem-Solution Story

▶ **Focus** This story challenges readers to separate pertinent from extraneous details and develop a logical solution to a given problem.

▶ **Teaching Tips**

Before Reading

- Discuss the meaning of the expression "think outside the box." Talk about the idea that details may seem hidden if they are not directly stated.

During Reading

- If students are not familiar with the word *dinghy*, encourage them to use contextual clues to figure out its meaning.
- It may help students to cross out extraneous details as they read and highlight key points they need to keep in mind.

After Reading

- Have students use this passage as a model to write their own problem-solution stories, then challenge classmates to use logic to solve them.

Common Core Connections

RL.6.1, RL.6.2, RL.6.3, RL.6.4, RL.6.5, RL.6.6, RL.6.10 • W.6.9, W.6.10 • L.6.1, L.6.2, L.6.3, L.6.4, L.6.5, L.6.6

Complexity Index

Quantitative: Lexile 1060

Qualitative	1	2	3	4	5
Meaning				✳	
Structure			✳		
Language			✳		
Knowledge		✳			

Reader & Task

- Students must employ analytical thinking skills and careful, critical reading to develop a solution to this non-routine problem.
- Invite students to share their solutions. Talk about what details were "hidden" and how the solution that meets all the criteria given involves more trips across and back than students may first have imagined.

Literature: Historical Fiction

▶ **Focus** Readers explore setting and cause-and-effect relationships in this fictional account of an actual journey that uses colorful, precise descriptions, nautical terms, and geographic detail.

▶ **Teaching Tips**

Before Reading

- Provide background on Magellan and his voyage of discovery. If possible, show images of sailing ships from that time.

During Reading

- Guide readers to highlight descriptive phrases and specific nautical terms to look up as needed, and to reread sentences or paragraphs to visualize the many details.

After Reading

- Have students cite details from the passage that show the effects caused by particular events.
- Challenge students to conduct research to find a nonfiction article about Magellan's discovery of the strait named after him, and then write an essay in which they compare and contrast the passage's viewpoint of this historic accomplishment with that in the story.

Common Core Connections

RL.6.1, RL.6.2, RL.6.3, RL.6.4, RL.6.5, RL.6.6, RL.6.10 • W.6.9, W.6.10 • L.6.1, L.6.2, L.6.3, L.6.4, L.6.5, L.6.6

Complexity Index

Quantitative:
Lexile 1070

Qualitative	1	2	3	4	5
Meaning			✳		
Structure			✳		
Language				✳	
Knowledge					✳

Reader & Task

- Exploration and life at sea in the 16th century will likely be unfamiliar to most readers.
- Understanding the distinction between a nonfiction historical account and a fictional one may be challenging for some students.
- Remind students that historical fiction is made-up but built around verifiable facts. Have them highlight phrases or sentences they believe may be factual, and then confirm their assumptions through research.

Passage 10 · Private Eye · page 44

Informational Text: Word Origin Article

▶ **Focus** This article presents detailed information chronologically to help students understand the etymology of a familiar expression.

▶ **Teaching Tips**

Before Reading
- Introduce the term *etymology* (the study of word or phrase origins).
- Preview and pronounce the word *surveillance* [sir-VAY-lehns].

During Reading
- Direct students to highlight unfamiliar words or phrases. Encourage them to use context clues to figure them out wherever possible.

After Reading
- Brainstorm a list of familiar phrases or words and invite students to guess their origins. Then challenge students to consult dictionaries and/or online sources for confirmation.

Common Core Connections

RI.6.1, RI.6.2, RI.6.3, RI.6.4, RI.6.5, RI.6.6, RI.6.7, RI.6.10 • W.6.9, W.6.10 • L.6.1, L.6.2, L.6.3, L.6.4, L.6.5, L.6.6

Complexity Index

Quantitative: Lexile 940

Qualitative	1	2	3	4	5
Purpose		✳			
Structure	✳				
Language			✳		
Knowledge			✳		

Reader & Task

- English language learners may have difficulty understanding the meaning of familiar expressions because they are usually not literal.
- Use the question that precedes the passage to have students discuss how the author builds a case for the origin of the expression *private eye*.

Passage 11 · A Writer's Story · page 46

Informational Text: Author Interview

▶ **Focus** By reading an interview, students have the opportunity to make connections between an author's life experiences and his career.

▶ **Teaching Tips**

Before Reading
- Review the elements of an interview. Focus on the kinds of questions that would elicit the most honest, detailed, and informative responses.
  (Note: This interview is excerpted from a longer interview with Laurence Yep on the Scholastic Teachers website.)

During Reading
- Point out to students that direct quotations are usually shown within quotation marks; sometimes, however, especially if they are long, quotations can be italicized, as they are in this piece.

After Reading
- Display some titles by Laurence Yep. Invite students who have read any of them to offer commentary and feedback. Encourage students to pick one to read and challenge them to look for evidence of the author they have come to know.

Common Core Connections

RI.6.1, RI.6.2, RI.6.3, RI.6.4, RI.6.5, RI.6.6, RI.6.7, RI.6.10 • W.6.9, W.6.10 • L.6.1, L.6.2, L.6.3, L.6.4, L.6.5, L.6.6

Complexity Index

Quantitative: Lexile 950

Qualitative	1	2	3	4	5
Purpose		✳			
Structure		✳			
Language		✳			
Knowledge		✳			

Reader & Task

- Some students may relate to Yep's feelings of being part of two worlds. Others may have experienced escaping into the imaginary worlds of literature.
- Have students make connections between Yep's early experiences in life and his professional pursuits as an adult.

Informational Text: Botany Essay

▶ **Focus** This detail-rich essay focuses readers on specific vocabulary, word study, author's purpose, and the effectiveness of a given position.

▶ **Teaching Tips**

Before Reading
- Tell students that although the essay contains long and challenging words, many include familiar parts to which readers can apply word-study skills to unlock meaning (for example, *instantaneously* and *epicenter*).

During Reading
- Suggest that students pause after each paragraph to look back to be sure they grasp its main idea and recall the most significant details.
- Instruct students to highlight evidence in the text that provides support for the author's position about the ginkgo.

After Reading
- Have students do research to examine the interconnectedness of earth's living things in the face of natural and human-caused changes, such as hurricanes, tsunamis, global warming, rain forest deforestation, and different kinds of pollution.

Common Core Connections

RI.6.1, RI.6.2, RI.6.3, RI.6.4, RI.6.5, RI.6.6, RI.6.7, RI.6.8, RI.6.10 • W.6.9, W.6.10 • L.6.1, L.6.2, L.6.3, L.6.4, L.6.5, L.6.6

Complexity Index

Quantitative: Lexile 960

Qualitative	1	2	3	4	5
Purpose			✳		
Structure		✳			
Language			✳		
Knowledge			✳		

Reader & Task

- The historical detail in the opening paragraph may disturb students. However, it provides background information to support the writer's position about the ginkgo biloba.
- Ask a volunteer to read aloud the closing paragraph of the essay. Have students respond to the question posed at the end, using details from the text to support their views.

Informational Text: Popular Culture Essay

▶ **Focus** This essay argues an unexpected position for students to consider and evaluate.

▶ **Teaching Tips**

Before Reading
- Brainstorm a list of superheroes students know. Then ask: *What about these superheroes makes people look up to them?* Discuss.

During Reading
- Ask students to describe how the layout of the text in this passage relates to its content.
- Suggest that students circle key words or ideas and reread sentences or paragraphs as needed to ensure that they fully grasp the author's point of view.

After Reading
- Invite students to pick a superhero they know well. Have them relate the essay's conclusion about the value of superheroes to the hero they chose, and be prepared to defend their viewpoint.

Common Core Connections

RI.6.1, RI.6.2, RI.6.3, RI.6.4, RI.6.5, RI.6.6, RI.6.8, RI.6.10 • W.6.9, W.6.10 • L.6.1, L.6.2, L.6.3, L.6.4, L.6.5, L.6.6

Complexity Index

Quantitative: Lexile 970

Qualitative	1	2	3	4	5
Purpose			✳		
Structure			✳		
Language			✳		
Knowledge		✳			

Reader & Task

- Students may never have analyzed superheroes beyond appreciating their entertainment value and eye-popping powers and gadgets.
- Have students work in groups to discuss similarities among, and differences between, the superheroes mentioned in the essay.

Informational Text: Biographical Sketch

▶ **Focus** Readers understand a person's character and motivation using background information and direct quotations.

▶ **Teaching Tips**

Before Reading

- Prepare students by explaining that they will read about someone who has not let her physical limitations keep her from living a rich and full life.

During Reading

- Ask students to explain the purpose of the sidebar in this passage. How does this information help the reader?
- Ask students to explain why the word *it* is in brackets (line 58).

After Reading

- Revisit Geri Jewell's quotation about adversity (lines 26–30). Then have students debate this point of view.
- If possible, view an online video clip of Geri Jewell speaking or performing.

Common Core Connections

RI.6.1, RI.6.2, RI.6.3, RI.6.4, RI.6.5, RI.6.6, RI.6.8, RI.6.10 • W.6.9, 6.10 • L.6.1, L.6.2, L.6.3, L.6.4, L.6.5, L.6.6

Complexity Index

Quantitative:
Lexile 980

Qualitative	1	2	3	4	5
Purpose			✳		
Structure			✳		
Language			✳		
Knowledge			✳		

Reader & Task

- Many students will be familiar with various physical challenges but may not know specifically about cerebral palsy.
- Encourage students to explicate two of the quotations used in this piece to demonstrate comprehension of Geri Jewell's character.

Informational Text: History Essay

▶ **Focus** This essay requires students to draw inferences from text evidence and a first-hand account of an American immigration experience.

▶ **Teaching Tips**

Before Reading

- Students may need support with content-specific vocabulary. You may wish to preview key terms, such as *interrogated*, *deport*, *exclusion*, and *barracks*.

During Reading

- Instruct students to identify cause-and-effect relationships as they read.
- Encourage readers to find connections between the essay and the personal recollection.

After Reading

- Invite students to list questions about the Angel Island experience, regarding such topics as daily routines and treatment, food, schooling, health care, and communication. Extend by having them research answers to their questions.

Common Core Connections

RI.6.1, RI.6.2, RI.6.3, RI.6.4, RI.6.5, RI.6.6, RI.6.10 • W.6.9, 6.10 • L.6.1, L.6.2, L.6.3, L.6.4, L.6.5, L.6.6

Complexity Index

Quantitative:
Lexile 990

Qualitative	1	2	3	4	5
Purpose			✳		
Structure			✳		
Language			✳		
Knowledge			✳		

Reader & Task

- Many students will relate to the challenges of being an immigrant. The topic of immigrant detention may be troubling for students.
- Have students describe the attitudes toward and treatment of immigrants at Angel Island using evidence from the text.

Passage 16 Game of Change • page 56

Informational Text: Sports History Essay

▶ **Focus** This essay lets students compare and contrast social and moral values, explore character, and evaluate the significance of an historic event.

▶ **Teaching Tips**

Before Reading

- Provide background, if needed, on the civil rights struggles of the 1960s in America. Clarify sports terms, as needed.
- Preview some of the essay's many multisyllabic words, including *elimination, predominantly, enthusiastic, acknowledged, segregationist, obstruction,* and *uniformly,* and encourage students to break them apart for comprehension.

During Reading

- Instruct students to scan the piece before close reading and notice how the subheadings help to organize the chronological structure.
- Suggest that students keep a T-chart to help them compare and contrast the two college teams and their supporters.

After Reading

- Discuss the meaning and impact of *reconciliation* 50 years after a dramatic event. Guide interested students to research integration in sports in America.

Common Core Connections

RI.6.1, RI.6.2, RI.6.3, RI.6.4, RI.6.5, RI.6.6, RI.6.8, RI.6.10 • W.6.9, W.6.10 • L.6.1, L.6.2, L.6.3, L.6.4, L.6.5, L.6.6

Complexity Index

Quantitative: Lexile 1000

Qualitative	1	2	3	4	5
Purpose				✳	
Structure		✳			
Language				✳	
Knowledge				✳	

Reader & Task

- Students who lack familiarity with the American civil-rights struggles of the 1960s may not realize the significance of the "Game of Change."
- Sports terms and references will make this passage more accessible to students who follow basketball but less so for others.
- Have students discuss attitudes about race in the 1960s and describe how this sporting event effected change.

Passage 17 Preserving Audio Archives • page 58

Informational Text: Speech

▶ **Focus** Through this speech, filled with statistical and historical data, students identify the argument for preserving cultural artifacts.

▶ **Teaching Tips**

Before Reading

- Draw attention to the title of the speech as well as the photographs and caption that accompany it. Have students predict what kinds of information the speech may present.

During Reading

- Encourage students to reread sentences, pause to process new information, and then highlight portions of the text that reflect the speaker's reasons for preserving audio archives.

After Reading

- Invite students to listen to archival recordings of music, speeches, or literary works available on the website of The Library of Congress.

Common Core Connections

RI.6.1, RI.6.2, RI.6.3, RI.6.4, RI.6.5, RI.6.6, RI.6.7, RI.6.10 • W.6.9, W.6.10 • L.6.1, L.6.2, L.6.3, L.6.4, L.6.5, L.6.6

Complexity Index

Quantitative: Lexile 1010

Qualitative	1	2	3	4	5
Purpose				✳	
Structure			✳		
Language				✳	
Knowledge				✳	

Reader & Task

- Students will likely be unfamiliar with the historical methods and formats of sound recording.
- Have students share their responses to question 6 (page 59) to identify the reasons put forth by the speaker for preserving audio archives.

Informational Text: Architecture/History Essay

▶ **Focus** This essay requires students to follow the cause-and-effect relationship between an urban disaster and a subsequent revitalization.

▶ **Teaching Tips**

Before Reading

- Read aloud the question that precedes the passage. Then share with students that, in Greek mythology, the phoenix was a rare bird that was reborn and "rose from the ashes" after fire destroyed it and its nest. Discuss the origin and meaning of this metaphor. Tell students to keep this information in mind as they read the passage.

During Reading

- Have students read the entire piece through quickly to get a general sense. Then have them go back and reread it slowly to absorb its many details and make connections among them.
- Explain to students that the actual cause of the Chicago fire is unknown.
- Draw students' attention to the photograph and caption. Ask: *Why does the author use the word* skeleton *to describe how the building was constructed?*

After Reading

- Tell students that by 1909, Chicago had earned the nickname "Paris on the Prairie." Discuss the possible meanings of that label. Extend by having students take an online tour of Chicago's past and present architecture.

Common Core Connections

RI.6.1, RI.6.2, RI.6.3, RI.6.4, RI.6.5, RI.6.6, RI.6.7, RI.6.8, RI.6.10 • W.6.9, W.6.10 • L.6.1, L.6.2, L.6.3, L.6.4, L.6.5, L.6.6

Complexity Index

Quantitative: Lexile 1020

Qualitative	1	2	3	4	5
Purpose				✳	
Structure			✳		
Language				✳	
Knowledge				✳	

Reader & Task

- Students may not recognize the significance of the shift to steel-frame construction.
- Some figurative language may challenge readers.
- Have students create a "Before and After" chart in which they list details describing Chicago's buildings before the 1871 fire and after.

Informational Text: Science/History Essay

▶ **Focus** This essay demands that students read and integrate technical and historical terms, recall details, note time sequence, and determine author's purpose.

▶ **Teaching Tips**

Before Reading

- Preview challenging science terms essential to understanding the essay, including *rocketry, combustion,* and *propulsion*. Also, pronounce *alchemist* (AL-keh-mist) and explain that *saltpeter* is the common name for potassium nitrate, a chemical used in rocket propellants and fireworks.

During Reading

- Tell students to pause to visualize each scenario—the pigeon on the wire, the "ground rat," and the "flying fire lances."
- Encourage students to consult a dictionary to find the meanings of unfamiliar words.

After Reading

- Discuss the new ideas students learned from this essay. Invite interested students to do further research into early rocketry.

Common Core Connections

RI.6.1, RI.6.2, RI.6.3, RI.6.4, RI.6.5, RI.6.6, RI.6.7, RI.6.10 • W.6.9, W.6.10 • L.6.1, L.6.2, L.6.3, L.6.4, L.6.5, L.6.6

Complexity Index

Quantitative: Lexile 1030

Qualitative	1	2	3	4	5
Purpose				✳	
Structure				✳	
Language				✳	
Knowledge					✳

Reader & Task

- Students may struggle with difficult scientific vocabulary and with historical information presented out of chronological order.
- Have students recount the chronological order of the key events described in the essay.

Passage 20 · Surprises in Ice · page 64

Informational Text: Environmental Science Article/Graph

▶ **Focus** This article requires students to read carefully and critically to draw conclusions about new data on climate science by analyzing information on a graph, noting cause-and-effect relationships, and making inferences.

▶ **Teaching Tips**

Before Reading
- Brainstorm what students already know or have heard about atmospheric gases and climate change.
- Preview challenging vocabulary, such as *potent, emissions, untainted, pristine, atmosphere, concentrations,* and *metallurgy.*

During Reading
- Encourage students to highlight technical terms to investigate further.
- Help students analyze the information on the graph, as needed.

After Reading
- Direct students to summarize the article by writing a user-friendly lab report with these bullet points: *Background, Hypothesis, Procedure, Results, Analysis, Conclusion.*

Common Core Connections

RI.6.1, RI.6.2, RI.6.3, RI.6.4, RI.6.5, RI.6.6, RI.6.7, RI.6.8, RI.6.10 • W.6.9, W.6.10
• L.6.1, L.6.2, L.6.3, L.6.4, L.6.5, L.6.6

Complexity Index

Quantitative:
Lexile 1040

Qualitative	1	2	3	4	5
Purpose				✳	
Structure				✳	
Language					✳
Knowledge					✳

Reader & Task

- Students will encounter abstract concepts and content-area vocabulary requiring careful, close reading, and calling for much support.
- Have students summarize the relationship between increases in farming and industry and methane gas levels.

Passage 21 · Astronomers' Desert · page 66

Informational Text: Geography/Science Article

▶ **Focus** This article demands that readers navigate lengthy sentences of differing structures to process chunks of new information about a little-known region of the world.

▶ **Teaching Tips**

Before Reading
- Help students locate the Atacama Desert on a map of South America.
- Review the attributes of a desert environment.

During Reading
- Suggest that students jot down questions that the text brings to mind for later discussion or research.
- Suggest that readers break long sentences into smaller chunks to aid comprehension.
- Tell students that ALMA stands for Atacama Large Millimeter/submillimeter Array. Ask them how this name relates to what they see in the photograph. (ALMA consists of an array of antennae.)

After Reading
- Discuss the irony of the next to last sentence in the article.

Common Core Connections

RI.6.1, RI.6.2, RI.6.3, RI.6.4, RI.6.5, RI.6.6, RI.6.7, RI.6.8, RI.6.10 • W.6.9, W.6.10
• L.6.1, L.6.2, L.6.3, L.6.4, L.6.5, L.6.6

Complexity Index

Quantitative:
Lexile 1050

Qualitative	1	2	3	4	5
Purpose				✳	
Structure			✳		
Language				✳	
Knowledge					✳

Reader & Task

- Students may find it challenging to visualize the Atacama environment and have little knowledge of the requirements of a world-class observatory.
- Have students use specific text references to justify why the author calls the Atacama an "astronomers' desert."

Informational Text: Art Essay

▶ **Focus** In this essay, students learn about a community project by reading historical and descriptive information, direct quotations, and examining a related photograph.

▶ **Teaching Tips**

Before Reading

- Discuss examples of large-form murals or other public artworks student have seen.

During Reading

- Point out to students that direct quotations in a text can be shown in different ways (for example, in block form and embedded in the text).
- Tell students to refer to the photograph to clarify descriptions they read in the essay.
- Ask students to explain why the word *this* is in brackets (line 20) and the purpose of the ellipsis (line 34).

After Reading

- Brainstorm questions students might have about the Mural Makers or members of SPARC in response to details from the essay. Extend by helping students find additional images of and information about this art project.

Common Core Connections

RI.6.1, RI.6.2, RI.6.3, RI.6.4, RI.6.5, RI.6.6, RI.6.7, RI.6.10 • W.6.9, W.6.10 • L.6.1, L.6.2, L.6.3, L.6.4, L.6.5, L.6.6

Complexity Index

Quantitative: Lexile 1050

Qualitative	1	2	3	4	5
Purpose		✳			
Structure			✳		
Language			✳		
Knowledge			✳		

Reader & Task

- Students from diverse backgrounds may be especially motivated by this essay and may wish to learn more about the project.
- Have students discuss the following question: *According to this essay, what else can art provide to a community beyond decoration?*

Informational Text: e-mail Business Letter

▶ **Focus** This letter enables students to identify the details and organization of a business letter and consider its tone and effectiveness.

▶ **Teaching Tips**

Before Reading

- Review the parts and functions of business letters and how and why they differ from friendly letters.

During Reading

- Guide students to read the entire letter first for its main idea, and then reread it more slowly and carefully to gather specific details and overall tone.
- This passage contains words with prefixes and suffixes (for example, *unpalatable*, *disappointment*, *underwhelmed*, *courteous*, *tasteless*). Suggest that students highlight them for analysis during reading.

After Reading

- Extend by inviting students to write a response to Julia from the manager based on details in the letter.

Common Core Connections

RI.6.1, RI.6.2, RI.6.3, RI.6.4, RI.6.5, RI.6.6, RI.6.8, RI.6.10 • W.6.9, W.6.10 • L.6.1, L.6.2, L.6.3, L.6.4, L.6.5, L.6.6

Complexity Index

Quantitative: Lexile 1060

Qualitative	1	2	3	4	5
Purpose		✳			
Structure		✳			
Language				✳	
Knowledge			✳		

Reader & Task

- Students may find the tone of the letter surprising and its approach unclear.
- Discuss the question that precedes the passage. Then ask students what the writer does *not* include (for example, insults, threats, requests for a remedy).

Informational Text: Letter to the Editor

▶ **Focus** This problem-solution letter requires students to understand an issue and to analyze the tone and effectiveness of the writer's argument.

▶ **Teaching Tips**

Before Reading

- Explain that communities may enact local laws regarding pets and public safety, such as leash laws, licensing regulations, and clean-up codes.
- Review the function of a letter-to-the-editor column in a newspaper or magazine.

During Reading

- Suggest that students take notes as they read to organize the argument into its parts: the writer's statement of the issue, views pro and con, suggestions, and conclusions.

After Reading

- Discuss the effectiveness of the letter. Focus on clarity, fairness to interested parties, tone, organization, knowledge of the issue, and reasonableness of suggestions.

Common Core Connections

RI.6.1, RI.6.2, RI.6.3, RI.6.4, RI.6.5, RI.6.6, RI.6.8, RI.6.10 • W.6.9, W.6.10 • L.6.1, L.6.2, L.6.3, L.6.4, L.6.5, L.6.6

Complexity Index

Quantitative: Lexile 1060

Qualitative	1	2	3	4	5
Purpose			✳		
Structure			✳		
Language		✳			
Knowledge		✳			

Reader & Task

- Students who do not live in urban areas may be unfamiliar with leash laws and with the many ways public spaces are shared.
- Have students write a brief character sketch of Madison Rosen based on the letter she wrote to the editor.

Informational Text: Technical Writing/Game Guide

▶ **Focus** This example of technical writing requires readers to sort through numerical and descriptive data to understand the specifications and rules for a sport and its equipment.

▶ **Teaching Tips**

Before Reading

- Tell students that table tennis is the official name of a sport they may know as Ping-Pong (a trademarked name for the sport).

During Reading

- Encourage students to refer to the illustration of the table for clarification as they read the game guide.

After Reading

- Have students compare and contrast this example of technical writing with the kind that gives steps to follow in a recipe or instructions for building a model.

Common Core Connections

RI.6.1, RI.6.2, RI.6.3, RI.6.4, RI.6.5, RI.6.6, RI.6.7, RI.6.10 • W.6.9, W.6.10 • L.6.1, L.6.2, L.6.3, L.6.4, L.6.5, L.6.6

Complexity Index

Quantitative: Lexile 1070

Qualitative	1	2	3	4	5
Purpose		✳			
Structure			✳		
Language			✳		
Knowledge			✳		

Reader & Task

- Students may find it challenging to navigate so much specific and numerical data presented all at once.
- Discuss what elements of the game guide make it both easy and difficult to read and use.

Name _____ Date _____

Gym Jam

Why does Kevin's invitation affect Mikayla so strongly?

1   It's challenging enough starting seventh
2   grade at a new school. But for the past
3   month, Mikayla found herself a reluctant
4   newcomer in a strange city more than a
5   thousand miles from where she'd lived
6   her whole life. She could barely name the
7. streets between her house and Ashland
8   Middle School. Seventh grade seemed
9   agreeable enough, most of her teachers
10 were reasonable, and her three-story school
11 was better equipped and more spacious
12 than the one back in Oneida. Still, Mikayla
13 was exhausted from the never-ending
14 getting accustomed to things.
15   Mikayla's newbie noggin was awhirl with sensory overload. She knew few
16 middle-school kids well enough to confide in, but knew how deeply she longed
17 for friendships. Not surprisingly, it felt like most of her classmates had been
18 together since kindergarten and few had extended welcomes to her. Most
19 seemed occupied enough with their own concerns to notice Mikayla's isolation.
20   Even when lonely, Mikayla could always raise her spirits by singing. She sang
21 along to the radio, TV, and her MP3 player. She crooned in the shower, warbled
22 through chores, hummed on the bus, and even serenaded her disinterested cats.
23 But singing alone was less gratifying than singing in an ensemble.
24   At the close of a particularly strenuous Monday, Mikayla bumped into Kevin
25 Stokes at their neighboring lockers. "Mikayla, you free tomorrow afternoon? It's
26 our first Gym Jam of the season, and we're hoping for a maximum crowd."
27   "Thanks for asking, Kevin, but I'm a pathetic athlete."
28   "Gym Jam's not about sports, it's about music," Kevin responded. "I've heard
29 you sing, so I consider you a likely suspect! Bet you didn't know that Coach
30 Tanaka played drums in a band during college. Every Tuesday, she sets up
31 her drum kit in the gym for a vocal jam with kids who love to sing. Nobody
32 auditions; interested singers just show up. She teaches us old rock songs with
33 arrangements for at least two parts, often three. Occasionally she recruits some
34 of us as back-up singers! We do harmonies, dance moves, and vocal sound
35 effects. It's crazy awesome!"
36   Mikayla couldn't believe how perfect this invitation sounded. "I play guitar,
37 Kev, so should I bring it?"
38   "Couldn't hurt," he said. "But maybe you should just show up this first time
39 and see how a Gym Jam goes. Do you sing high, medium, or low?"
40   "You bring it, I sing it!" Mikayla chanted, and raced with Kevin toward
41 the bus.

25 Complex Text Passages to Meet the Common Core: Literature and Informational Texts, Grade 6 © 2014 by Scholastic Teaching Resources

Name _____ Date _____

Gym Jam

▶ **Answer each question. Give evidence from the story.**

1 Which is *not* one of Mikayla's impressions of her new classmates?

○ A. Most acted concerned with their own issues.   ○ C. Most had not reached out to her.

○ B. Most seemed to have been together for years.   ○ D. Most were active and athletic.

How did you determine your response? _____

_____

_____

2 Which best describes something that is *awhirl* (line 15)?

○ A. It feels painful.   ○ C. It feels empty and sad.

○ B. It feels dizzying.   ○ D. It feels heavy and solid.

What evidence in the text helped you answer? _____

_____

_____

3 Describe Mikayla's way to cheer herself up. _____

_____

_____

4 What was so perfect about Kevin's invitation? Explain. _____

_____

_____

5 How did Mikayla's attitude change after hearing about the Gym Jam? _____

_____

_____

6 Explain why Mikayla misunderstood Kevin's offer at first. _____

_____

_____

Name _____ Date _____

The Golden Axe

Based on a Fable by Aesop

What details suggest that this story is a fable?

1   A humble woodcutter chopped trees daily in the
2 forest. Late one afternoon, he chose his final tree,
3 which stood beside a deep green pool. The strokes
4 the weary woodcutter took were less accurate than
5 usual. After a mighty swing, his trusty axe slipped
6 from his grip, flew headfirst into the water, and
7 disappeared into the green abyss.
8   "Woe unto me!" he bellowed. The axe was his
9 only possession with which to earn a living; he
10 lacked the money to obtain another. But he could
11 neither swim nor dive to retrieve his axe from
12 such depths. As he shed bitter tears, the winged
13 god Mercury suddenly appeared to investigate his
14 misery. Embarrassed, the woodcutter explained
15 how he lost his axe.
16   Instantly, Mercury plunged deep into the pool to recover the drowned axe.
17 But the axe Mercury retrieved was made of glittering gold. "Is this your axe?"
18 the god asked.
19   The truthful woodcutter replied, "No, kind Mercury. That axe is wonderful
20 beyond description, but it's not mine." Mercury set the gold axe on the
21 ground and dove again to the depths of the pool. Now he retrieved an axe of
22 shimmering silver. Again, the sincere woodman thanked the winged god, but
23 described his axe as an ordinary iron tool with a well-worn wooden handle.
24   So Mercury dove a third time, returning with the axe the woodcutter had
25 lost. "My axe!" he cried in gratitude. "This modest tool enables me to earn
26 my living; without it I'd be lost. My deepest thanks, O Mercury."
27   Accepting the woodcutter's appreciation, the god said, "Because I admire
28 your honesty, you may possess all three axes—the gold, the silver, and your
29 own." The astonished woodcutter knelt to Mercury and then trekked home
30 with the three axes.
31   Accounts of the woodcutter's good fortune spread rapidly. Other
32 woodcutters believed that they could increase their wealth by losing an axe—
33 or pretending to—and appealing to Mercury for divine help. One by one,
34 other woodcutters hid their axes in bushes, caves, or deep bodies of water,
35 and wailed for Mercury's assistance.
36   Winged Mercury appeared to investigate each man's plight. Each time,
37 Mercury displayed an axe of glistening gold, which the man excitedly
38 claimed as the one he'd unfortunately lost. But instead of "returning" the
39 gold axe, Mercury used it to deliver to the deceitful woodcutter's head a sharp
40 thwack, sending him home in pain, but without any axe at all.

Name _____ Date _____

The Golden Axe

▶ **Answer each question. Give evidence from the fable.**

1 The pool in the forest was an *abyss* (line 7) because it was very _____.

○ A. green ○ B. clear ○ C. deep ○ D. cool

What evidence in the text helped you answer? _____

_____

_____

2 Which of the following is the most reasonable moral for this story?

○ A. Honesty is the best policy. ○ C. Things aren't always as they seem.

○ B. One good turn deserves another. ○ D. A pool may not always return lost tools.

How did you determine your response? _____

_____

_____

3 Why was the woodcutter's axe handle so well-worn? _____

_____

_____

4 Explain why the woodcutter felt embarrassed (line 14). _____

_____

_____

5 How would you describe the character of Mercury? _____

_____

_____

6 What makes a story a fable? Explain. _____

_____

_____

_____

Name _____ Date _____

Sounds of Spring

What strategies does the writer use to make readers laugh?

1 All the ballplayers had reported to camp,
2 and March was around the corner. The
3 familiar sounds of baseball—*Crack! Thump!*
4 *Smack! Ouch!*—echoed in the dry desert air
5 of southern Arizona. It was spring training,
6 and all Major League teams were gearing
7 up for the new season. Those characteristic
8 spring training noises are actually the ones I
9 typically make. I'm a seasoned catcher's mitt.
10 From my exalted position behind home
11 plate, I observe it all—outfielders shagging
12 flies, infielders taking grounders, pitchers
13 throwing at catchers' mitts with all their
14 might. Just then a massive young flame-
15 thrower eager to snare a place on the big-
16 league roster lumbers to the red dirt of the
17 pitcher's mound. He has every intention of
18 throwing that rock-solid little ball at me as
19 fast as he can. I sigh, open my eyes wide, and
20 brace myself for the impact of a bullet train.
21 And what an impact! Ooh, that stung! Catching a 95-mph fastball smarts,
22 despite all the padding I have. By the way, I get no sympathy from those spoiled
23 outfielder gloves as big as bushel baskets, nor even from those infielder gloves
24 with the generous, forgiving webbing. "Stop your whining!" they scold. "Come
25 back here and try it yourself!" I retort. To my mind, any glove should grasp that
26 I'm in a particularly punishing situation for three exhausting hours at a time.
27 I await the next pitch with apprehension. The burly hurler winds up, and
28 the cannonball hurtles my way at the speed of light. I grimace, waiting for
29 the imminent impact. Good news! The ball sails wide left, the catcher misses
30 it altogether, and I am pain-free for the moment. I know, however, that my
31 fortune can't last and just hope that the catcher will start calling for slow curves
32 or change-ups. The difference between a 95-mph heater and a 75-mph pitch,
33 you see, is the difference between a searing pain and a throbbing ache.
34 This spring training day ends like the others, with me, sore from seam to
35 seam, tossed heedlessly into a yawning locker to lick my wounds. Alas, I know
36 that the following day will bring more of the same distress.
37 But just as I am settling into a substantial sulk, the next day's lineup is posted
38 where I can readily eyeball it from my metal cell. My catcher is not scheduled
39 to appear in the game! Oh, rapture! Oh, bliss! But then I glance underneath the
40 lineup to check assignments. To my dismay, he is assigned to warm up pitchers
41 in the bull pen. Have they no compassion?

Name _____ Date _____

Sounds of Spring

▶ **Answer each question. Give evidence from the monologue.**

1 What does the narrator mean by a *seasoned* (line 9) catcher's mitt?

○ A. a worn-out baseball glove   ○ C. a baseball glove used during spring training

○ B. a baseball glove used year round   ○ D. a baseball glove that has been used often

What evidence in the text helped you answer? _____

_____

_____

2 Based on the context, a *heater* (line 32) is _____.

○ A. a warming device   ○ C. a very fast pitch

○ B. a gentle pitch   ○ D. a pitch that travels exactly 95 mph

What evidence in the text helped you answer? _____

_____

_____

3 Who gives this monologue? Explain. _____

_____

_____

4 What is the *metal cell* (line 38) the narrator refers to? _____

_____

_____

5 What words would you use to describe the personality of the catcher's mitt? _____

_____

_____

6 How does the author create humor in this piece? _____

_____

_____

_____

Name _____ Date _____

What Goes Around…

Hindu Folktale

What details suggest that this story is a folktale?

1   As an elderly father approached death, he summoned his children.
2   "Treasured daughters, I have achieved great wealth; as I always provided for
3   you in life, so shall I continue after I depart this earth. Since my life will soon
4   conclude, I shall divide everything I have into three equitable shares—one for
5   each of you. When I have passed, you will receive a substantial inheritance,
6   empowering you to live in splendid security. I ask only for comfort in my final
7   days." Silently, the daughters nodded their agreement.
8   So the man divided his wealth into identical portions, but he greatly
9   misjudged his health and lived several years longer. Unfortunately, his extended
10   life was fraught with challenges. Alongside the fatigue and isolation of declining
11   health, he endured the sting of cold-heartedness. His daughters, once deeply
12   devoted and considerate, now engaged in petty squabbling and ignored their
13   father's needs.
14   "Wretched, greedy ingrates!" the old man lamented. "You girls once competed
15   to honor me—how gullible I was. You pretended to cherish me merely to ensure
16   robust inheritances! But with your futures determined, you care nothing for the
17   father who made it so, which torments my heart. To you my existence is but a
18   bothersome nuisance, a needless expense."
19   One day the father implored his wisest sister to visit to allow him to disclose
20   his anguish about his selfish, neglectful daughters. Sympathizing deeply, the
21   sister pledged to devise a strategy that would improve his situation. Several
22   days later, she returned, delivering six bulky, padlocked trunks for the family
23   to behold. The sister privately alerted her brother, "I formulated a plan that
24   should allow your days to pass unburdened. Inform your daughters that I
25   finally satisfied my long-standing
26   debt, thus adding thousands of rupees
27   and precious jewels to your fortune. I
28   believe this news will transform your
29   daughters' manners. But the trunks
30   must never be unlocked until after
31   your death." The solemn siblings
32   hugged in sober agreement.

33   When the daughters learned of their
34   father's amplified wealth, they swiftly
35   became more attentive than ever, and
36   maintained their helpfulness until his
37   demise. When they greedily pried open
38   the trunks, the daughters discovered
39   their deserved reward: gravel, sand,
40   and rocks.

Name _____ Date _____

What Goes Around...

▶ **Answer each question. Give evidence from the folktale.**

1 Which of the following is an antonym for *equitable* (line 4)?

○ A. even-handed   ○ B. dissimilar   ○ C. equivalent   ○ D. just

What evidence in the text helped you answer? _____

_____

_____

2 Why did the dying man fear that he had been *gullible* (line 15)?

○ A. He finally saw that his daughters cared only for his wealth.

○ B. He lived much longer than he ever expected he would.

○ C. He realized he had been greedy with his money.

○ D. He needed to approach his sister for help.

How did you determine your response? _____

_____

3 What is the elderly father's dying wish? _____

_____

4 Why did the daughters' honorable behavior toward their father change? _____

_____

_____

5 Explain how the six-trunk plan affected the man's daughters. _____

_____

_____

6 The title of this folktale is the first part of the saying "What goes around comes around." How does that saying apply to this story?

_____

_____

_____

_____

Name _____ Date _____

City in the Sky

In what ways is the setting of the piece its most important character?

1　　The drive west across the high desert
2　from Albuquerque to Acoma Pueblo
3　was breathtaking. The sky was the
4　bluest of blues, and the views of gray,
5　pale orange, and rust-red mesas in all
6　directions were awesome. New Mexico
7　truly appeared to live up to its moniker,
8　the "land of enchantment."

Acoma Pueblo

9　　The ancient "sky city" was our
10　destination. I'd read that we were about
11　to visit a unique community set atop a
12　367-foot sandstone mesa. This site has
13　been continually inhabited for more
14　than nine centuries.

15　　We parked at the Sky City Cultural
16　Center nestled at the foot of the mesa.
17　This modern structure was designed to resemble one of the 300 or so adobe
18　buildings on the mesa. It even had exterior ladders. Inside we learned about
19　Acoma Indian history and culture. We also received instructions in proper
20　visitor etiquette. For instance, taking photographs was restricted to those
21　willing to pay a fee.

22　　After wolfing down the best tamales ever, we trudged up a winding road to
23　the summit and the start of our tour. Although there was a bus ready to drive
24　us, Dad insisted that we hike to the top as the Acoma Indians had always
25　done. I pointed out that the road was new and that the earlier residents had
26　had to climb a challenging rock staircase.

27　　Arriving atop the mesa, we understood at once what a formidable fortress
28　Acoma was. Our guide, Leroy, pointed out that its defensive position once
29　protected the inhabitants from the intruding Spanish conquistadors, as well
30　as from other Indian groups in the region. He told us that the ancient village
31　is now home to fewer than 50 people. They live there without running water
32　or electricity. Hearing that they depend on visitors for some of their income, I
33　knew Mom was certain to buy a piece of distinctive Acoma pottery.

34　　Our last stop on the tour was the San Esteban del Rey mission. It is a
35　National Historical Landmark and the most prominent structure on the mesa.
36　This centuries-old adobe and wood church features designs representing both
37　Christian and indigenous beliefs. Leroy's father is one of the caretakers of the
38　mission. His job is a highly respected, lifelong commitment.

39　　By 9 P.M. we were back at our hotel, finished with dinner, and totally wiped
40　out. After all, our body clocks ticked midnight. I was asleep within seconds,
41　my *Guide to Santa Fe and Taos* resting on my chest.

Name _____ Date _____

City in the Sky

▶ **Answer each question. Give evidence from the travel piece.**

1 Which of the following is true about the Acoma Pueblo?

○ A. It is located in Albuquerque, New Mexico.

○ B. It has all the features of a modern community.

○ C. People have lived there for more than 900 years.

○ D. Its inhabitants encourage the taking of photographs.

What evidence in the text helped you answer? _____

_____

2 Which is another word for *moniker* (line 7)?

○ A. advertisement   ○ B. destination   ○ C. location   ○ D. nickname

What evidence in the text helped you answer? _____

_____

3 Why would the author say *trudged* (line 22) instead of *walked*? _____

_____

_____

4 Why might so few Acoma people live atop the mesa? _____

_____

_____

5 How do you know that the Acoma people value their mission? Explain. _____

_____

_____

_____

6 What inference can you make about the travelers by knowing that their "body clocks ticked midnight" (line 40)? Explain.

_____

_____

_____

Name _____ Date _____

Thief of Fire

Greek Myth

Why and how does Prometheus defy Zeus?

1   Prometheus was a Titan, a lesser god but still immortal. His master was Zeus,
2   king of all gods, who lived atop Mount Olympus. Zeus entrusted Prometheus
3   with the huge task of molding human beings out of water and dirt, which he
4   did. So proud was Prometheus of his efforts that he befriended the lowly mortals
5   he formed.
6   The mighty Zeus had no respect for mortals. He expected them to endure
7   short, crude lives, no better than animals. Zeus withheld all divine gifts from
8   the mortals for fear that any power they might attain could threaten him. He
9   commanded Prometheus to neglect his living creations.
10   But Prometheus had grown fond of the mortals. He wanted to teach them
11   the ways of civilization, but Zeus plainly forbade this. Prometheus realized that
12   Zeus lacked compassion for mortals. Against all warnings, Prometheus
13   disobeyed Zeus to help the mortals better their lives. First, he tricked
14   Zeus by interfering with the first sacrifice of an ox that mortals were
15   ordered to make to show their obedience. Prometheus set aside the
16   choicest meat for the mortals and sent only bones, teeth, skin, and
17   lesser parts to the gods. Zeus was outraged.
18   Prometheus secretly bestowed other gifts upon the mortals,
19   including bricks, saddles, precious metals, and healing plants.
20   But his ultimate act of defiance was to devise a plan to steal fire
21   from Zeus and share it with the mortals. The successful theft
22   of divine fire by Prometheus caused Zeus to explode into a
23   violent rage.
24   Zeus had Prometheus chained high upon the side of a
25   rocky cliff. Prometheus hung there, suspended in space
26   and time, enduring constant wrath. Every
27   day, Zeus sent a gigantic eagle to tear away
28   Prometheus's flesh and eat his liver. During
29   the night, all his painful wounds would
30   miraculously heal and his liver would regrow,
31   but the torture would begin anew at sunrise.
32   The fury of Zeus did not end with the suffering
33   of Prometheus. He vowed to penalize the entire mortal
34   world. His ambitious punishment would reverse every
35   good thing Prometheus had done. To accomplish this, Zeus
36   sought a hateful creature whose pleasing manner would
37   give way to a terrible storm of disease, hate, envy, and
38   mayhem, encircling all mortals. Zeus ordered the creation of
39   Pandora…

Name _____ Date _____

Thief of Fire

▶ **Answer each question. Give evidence from the myth.**

1 What made Prometheus befriend the mortals?

○ A. He wanted to figure out how to trick them.   ○ C. He hoped to become a mortal himself.

○ B. He felt proud of and responsible for them.   ○ D. He needed to figure out how they lived.

What evidence in the text helped you answer? _____

_____

_____

2 Why did Zeus demand that the mortals sacrifice an ox?

○ A. Zeus was king of the universe.   ○ C. Zeus expected mortals to obey him.

○ B. Zeus had no compassion for animals.   ○ D. Zeus was known for having a bad temper.

How did you determine your response? _____

_____

_____

3 Describe what it means to show *defiance* (line 20). Suggest another word that has a similar meaning.

_____

_____

4 What clues in the text might explain why Prometheus healed every night from his terrible wounds?

_____

_____

5 How would you describe Zeus? Write a brief character sketch of him. _____

_____

_____

6 Why does this myth end with the punctuation (…)? Explain the effect of this. _____

_____

_____

Name _____ Date _____

Out Back of Beyond

How does the author combine magical and realistic details in this story?

1   Liza gathered her gear and collected Tito for their weekly
2   Saturday hike on a little-used trail. The day's forecast
3   of cool breezes and clear skies promised a perfect
4   opportunity for an excursion out back of beyond.
5   At the trailhead, Liza and Tito filled their
6   canteens, adjusted their boots, and started
7   up the path into the woods. They chatted
8   and took snapshots, but mainly walked
9   in silence to appreciate their peaceful
10 surroundings.
11   After about an hour, the duo detected
12 the refreshing sound of a creek. Liza
13 sprinted ahead, eager to relax beside its
14 burbling water. Detecting a rotten smell
15 spoiling the freshness, she wrinkled her
16 nose, halted at creek-side, and stared ahead
17 in shock. On the opposite bank towered a hairy,
18 mud-spattered ape-like figure with elongated arms
19 and brawny legs. Gulping in disbelief, Liza whistled
20 for Tito, who rushed toward her, nearly toppling her. "Liza,
21 what's wrong?"
22   "Ssss…sasquatch! I saw Sasquatch," Liza gasped and pointed. As they
23 struggled to stay upright, the strange creature fled.
24   Tito scoffed and challenged Liza's outlandish claim. Shushing him
25 with a finger to her lips, Liza led the way as she and Tito crossed stepping
26 stones to the spot where Sasquatch had been. In the muddy bank, the
27 pair discovered 19-inch footprints—deep enough for a creature weighing
28 hundreds of pounds. The strides were easily seven feet apart.
29   Astonished but curious, Tito examined the ominous footprints while
30 Liza wondered who or what had made them. When Tito rose to follow the
31 prints, Liza wavered—she'd heard that Sasquatch occasionally lingered in
32 shadows to observe its prey.
33   "No more prints here," called Tito. "Maybe your Sasquatch is lurking
34 behind that boulder." Liza nodded at Tito, prepared to scream at any sign
35 of trouble when she caught another whiff of rotten garbage; she froze.
36 Tito tiptoed around the rock and came face to face with the monstrous
37 creature! He emitted a strangled cry as Sasquatch bellowed its own startled
38 howl. Tito and Liza dashed back across the creek as Sasquatch stood in
39 silence, then clambered away through the trees, trailing its stink.

Name _____ Date _____

Out Back of Beyond

▶ **Answer each question. Give evidence from the story.**

1 What was the first clue Liza detected that something was wrong?

○ A. They walked in silence.   ○ C. She saw the giant footprints.

○ B. She noticed a rotten smell.   ○ D. The weather was too perfect.

How did you determine your response? _____

_____

_____

2 Which is *not* a synonym for an *excursion* (line 4)?

○ A. an outing   ○ B. a jaunty walk   ○ C. a pleasure trip   ○ D. a wooded trail

What evidence in the text helped you answer? _____

_____

_____

3 Explain what was scary about the footprints Liza and Tito discovered. _____

_____

_____

4 How would you describe Tito? Summarize his character traits. _____

_____

_____

5 Reread the title. What hints does it provide about the passage? _____

_____

_____

6 What unexpected thing did Sasquatch do? How might you explain it? _____

_____

_____

_____

Name _____ Date _____

Dogs and a Dinghy

How can "hidden" information help you solve a problem?

1   Below is a fresh variation of a classic logic problem. Apply careful reading,
2 visualization, and modeling strategies to unearth its sensible, even elegant,
3 solution. Hint: You'll need to "think outside the box." Read the problem
4 thoroughly and imagine the situation just as it is presented, because it
5 provides all the facts you need, as well as some extraneous details.
6   Willa has three dogs—Mollie, Pastrami, and Teddy. Mollie is an impetuous
7 beagle pup, friendly and curious, feisty and fierce. Pastrami, named for Willa's
8 favorite sandwich, is a companionable golden retriever who adores water but
9 detests getting drenched to the skin. Teddy is the eldest of the group, a 12-year-
10 old English bulldog, part-deaf and altogether stubborn.
11   On this beautiful summer day, Willa and her three canines have been on
12 a ramble through scrubby, hilly woods. After about an hour they arrive at a
13 wide stream. The dogs eagerly drink from its cool water as Willa ponders how
14 to cross the stream so they can continue their stroll on the other side to visit a
15 popular lookout point.
16   Willa realizes that the depth of the stream is too great for the group to
17 wade across and, unlike their owner, the dogs are not competent swimmers.
18 Fortunately, a small dinghy is tethered to a tree on the near bank and Willa is
19 adept at rowing. Unfortunately, three significant complications present quite
20 the dilemma.

21   • The dinghy can safely hold Willa and only
22   one pooch.

23   • Mollie and Pastrami aren't the most
24   cooperative of friends. If left alone, the duo
25   will surely wind up in a doggy dustup, so
26   Willa cannot leave them unattended.

27   • Teddy and Mollie also antagonize
28   one another; leaving those two alone
29   together will swiftly result in a barking
30   competition that would disrupt the peaceful
31   surroundings. So Willa must avoid this
32   situation as well.

33   In a nutshell, you now have the details of
34 Willa's predicament. She must formulate a plan to
35 paddle all three dogs safely across the stream while
36 accounting for all of the above circumstances.
37 To help devise a resolution, she has sketched
38 a diagram. Imagine yourself in Willa's shoes,
39 needing to determine the best course of action.

Name _____ Date _____

Dogs and a Dinghy

▶ **Answer each question. Give evidence from the story.**

1 What problem must Willa solve?

○ A. how to make Teddy and Mollie stop barking so much

○ B. how to get all three dogs safely across a deep stream

○ C. how to find the shortest path to the lookout point

○ D. how to paddle a small boat all by herself

What evidence in the text helped you answer? _____

_____

2 Which is an example of an *extraneous* (line 5) detail?

○ A. Teddy is the oldest of Willa's three dogs.

○ B. Pastrami and Mollie cannot be left alone together.

○ C. The dinghy can safely hold only Willa and one dog.

○ D. Mollie and Teddy cannot stay together without Willa.

What evidence in the text helped you answer? _____

_____

3 Which facts about the dogs must Willa always keep in mind to plan her course of action?

_____

_____

4 Which pair of pooches *can* stay alone together? _____

5 The word *elegant* usually means stylish and graceful. What might the author mean by an *elegant solution* (lines 2 and 3)?

_____

_____

6 Describe the plan Willa can use to get the dogs across the stream. You can draw a diagram or use the illustration to help you.

_____

_____

_____

Name _____ Date _____

Ship's Boy

How does the writer bring this story to life?

1   As he stood on the *Trinidad*'s stern, 30 feet above the Guadalquivir River,
2   young Juan Cabrera tried to conceal his excitement. As the Captain's servant,
3   he wanted to look the part. It was August 10, 1519, when the five ships of
4   Magellan's *Armada de Molucca*, black from the tar smeared over their hulls,
5   masts, and riggings, left Seville. They were bound for the Atlantic and the
6   unknown.
7   Juan, just shy of his 12th birthday, was a ship's boy. While other boys his
8   age handled menial tasks, his assignment was to maintain the ship's sand
9   clocks by turning them every half-hour. It was an easy but essential task.
10   He could thank his father for arranging this privileged position on his very
11   first voyage.
12   A sailor's life, as Juan soon discovered, was rough, back-breaking, and
13   perilous. The ships were tossed about like toy boats. Juan cried helplessly
14   when the *Santiago*, with his cousin Rafael aboard, sank in a storm. But as
15   his father had advised him, Juan minded his manners and quietly observed
16   life on board to learn what he could. He listened as the sailors chanted while
17   hauling anchors, climbing masts, swabbing decks, or working the pumps. He
18   recognized a different chant for each task. And by eavesdropping when the
19   officers met in the Captain's cabin, he learned that Captain Magellan was
20   seeking a water passage through the Americas into the Pacific. This had never
21   before been done.
22   After fruitlessly exploring one promising river mouth after another
23   along the South American coast, the four remaining ships finally found the
24   waterway Magellan so desperately sought. When Juan flipped the sand clocks
25   on October 21, 1520, more than a year after they'd left Spain, the *Trinidad*
26   and the others entered the deep, frigid, uncharted waters of what would come
27   to be called the Strait of Magellan.
28   The strait was nearly always overcast, at once gloomy and awesome.
29   Iridescent blue walls of solid ice groaned and roared as chunks, some as big
30   as whales, tumbled into the water. Dark forests rose up behind rocky beaches
31   lined with elephant seals and penguins. Jagged snowy peaks disappeared in
32   the clouds, while giant condors wheeled in the mist.
33   Though the sights were majestic, the passage was terrifying. Magellan was
34   getting increasingly irritable, Juan noticed. Strong currents, high tides, narrow
35   channels, fierce winds, and violent gales explained it. After the *San Antonio*
36   mutinied and turned back, things got somber indeed. Only when the metallic
37   waters of the Pacific came into view a month later did the mood aboard the
38   *Trinidad* change. Juan did not refrain from smiling broadly when the Captain,
39   proud of his accomplishment, embraced him and said, "My boy, we are now
40   where none have been before. It's a fitting birthday gift, wouldn't you agree?"

Name _____ Date _____

Ship's Boy

▶ **Answer each question. Give evidence from the passage.**

1 Juan was *not* assigned *menial* (line 8) tasks on the ship. Which of the following is the best example of a *menial* task aboard a ship?

  ○ A. doing laundry   ○ C. repairing the ship's main sails

  ○ B. navigating by the stars   ○ D. writing entries in the ship's log

What evidence in the text helped you answer? _____

_____

2 Which best describes the passage through the Strait of Magellan?

  ○ A. It was swift and smooth but sometimes boring.   ○ C. It was dark, rocky, and blazing hot.

  ○ B. It was stormy, cold, scary, but amazing.   ○ D. It took over a year.

What evidence in the text helped you answer? _____

_____

_____

3 Describe some dangers sailors faced on Magellan's wooden ships. _____

_____

_____

4 How would you describe waters that are *uncharted* (line 26)? _____

_____

_____

5 What made Juan's job on the *Trinidad* so important? _____

_____

_____

6 How is this story an example of historical fiction? Explain. _____

_____

_____

_____

_____

Name _____ Date _____

Private Eye

How does the author build a case for where an expression came from?

1 Private investigators (PIs)
2 are detectives specially hired
3 for their skill at digging
4 up information. Attorneys
5 hire PIs to gather facts
6 that help them solve their
7 cases. Insurance companies
8 hire them to investigate
9 claims. And sometimes one
10 individual will hire a PI to
11 closely track someone else.
12   So where did the term
13 *private eye* come from?
14   Although spies have
15 been around for centuries,
16 the history of private
17 investigation can be traced
18 to agencies in France and Great Britain in the early-to-mid 19th century. But
19 the moniker private eye comes from America. It arrived with the emergence
20 of Allan Pinkerton's National Detective Agency.
21   Pinkerton came to the United States from Scotland and established his
22 agency in 1850. He quickly gained attention for his keen ability to track
23 down and apprehend outlaws. He earned a reputation for developing
24 innovative and creative surveillance techniques. For example, he introduced
25 the idea of circulating photos of criminals accompanied by detailed records
26 and descriptions. Pinkerton invented the *mug shot*.
27   Pinkerton is perhaps best known for foiling a plot by Baltimore
28 secessionists to assassinate President-Elect Abraham Lincoln on his way to
29 Washington. After that, his spy network served the Federal Army during the
30 Civil War. His exalted reputation dimmed a little during those years as his
31 assessments of the enemy's strength routinely turned out to be overestimates.
32 Nonetheless, his agency continued to prosper. After the war, he returned to
33 ferreting out law breakers. Jesse James, Butch Cassidy, and the Sundance Kid
34 were among his targets.
35   The façade of Pinkerton's National Detective Agency building in Chicago
36 displayed the company's logo. It was a large picture of a wide-open eye
37 embellished with the company's slogan: "We Never Sleep." This logo was the
38 likely source of the term private eye.

Name _____ Date _____

Private Eye

▶ **Answer each question. Give evidence from the article.**

1 From which country does the term *private eye* come?

○ A. France ○ B. Scotland ○ C. Chicago ○ D. United States

What evidence in the text helped you answer? _____

_____

_____

2 The word *façade* (line 35) is an architecture word. Which part of the Chicago building do you think it names?

○ A. the roof ○ B. the front ○ C. the office ○ D. the basement

What evidence in the text helped you answer? _____

_____

_____

3 Why do you think the author gave the term *mug shot* (line 26) in italics? _____

_____

_____

4 For what accomplishment is Allan Pinkerton most famous? _____

_____

_____

5 Why do you think the author made a paragraph with only one sentence (lines 12 and 13)? Explain.

_____

_____

6 Why might the slogan "We Never Sleep" encourage clients to use Pinkerton's National Detective Agency? Explain.

_____

_____

_____

Name _____ Date _____

A Writer's Story

How have Yep's life experiences influenced his writing?

1 Laurence Yep (b.1948) has written over 60
2 books for diverse audiences. Recipient of
3 prestigious honors and awards, this prolific
4 writer has produced novels, plays, picture
5 books, poetry, folktales, mysteries, fantasy,
6 and science fiction. He has also crafted an
7 autobiography and articles on a wide variety
8 of topics. Below are his answers to questions
9 students posed at an interview.

Laurence Yep

10 **What kinds of books did you like to read**
11 **as a child?**
12 *As a child, I read mostly science fiction and fantasy*
13 *books…I grew up in a black neighborhood but went*
14 *to school in Chinatown. So I moved back and forth*
15 *between two ghettoes. I could never get into the*
16 *Homer Price novels…in those books, every kid had a*
17 *bicycle, and every kid left their front door unlocked, and that was alien to me as a child. You*
18 *had to lock your doors, and no one I knew had a bike. But in science fiction and fantasy,*
19 *children leave the everyday world and go to a strange place where they have to learn a new*
20 *language and new customs. Science fiction and fantasy were about adapting, and that was*
21 *something I did every day when I got on and off the bus.*

22 **At what age did you start writing?**
23 *I started writing at the age of seventeen because I had a teacher in high school who said*
24 *that we had to get something accepted by a national magazine to get an A. The teacher*
25 *later withdrew that threat, but the writing bug bit me. …*

26 **Why do you write all of your books about Chinese culture?**
27 *It's what I know best, but I also write about other things.*

28 **Where do you get your ideas for your stories?**
29 *I get the ideas from everything. …good writing brings out what's special in ordinary*
30 *things. …writing only requires taking one step to the side and looking at something from*
31 *a slightly different angle.*

32 **Do you believe your creativity is based on a very active imagination?**
33 *I think it's part of being alive. …part of just being open to the world. We learn to shut*
34 *ourselves off from our feelings and our memories, and a writer learns how to connect all*
35 *those things together.*

Name _____ Date _____

A Writer's Story

▶ **Answer each question. Give evidence from the interview.**

1 What prevented Laurence Yep from getting into the Homer Price novels?

○ A. Homer Price was not a Chinese American.

○ B. Homer Price's life seemed completely alien to Yep.

○ C. Yep disliked stories about boys and bicycles.

○ D. The Homer Price books did not include enough fantasy.

How did you determine your response? _____

_____

_____

2 Why would a writer be described as *prolific* (line 3)?

○ A. The writer has won awards.   ○ C. The writer has written many books.

○ B. The writer is over 50 years old.   ○ D. The writer has become very famous.

What evidence in the text helped you answer? _____

_____

3 What prompted Yep's early interest in fantasy and science fiction? _____

_____

_____

4 What is the purpose of the ellipses (…) in this piece (lines 13, 16, 25, 29, and 33)? _____

_____

5 What does Yep mean when he recalls that "the writing bug bit me" (line 25)? _____

_____

_____

6 Yep believes that good writing "brings out what's special in ordinary things" (line 29). According to Yep, how do writers accomplish that?

_____

_____

_____

Name _____ Date _____

Ancient Survivor

What about the ginkgo makes it a remarkable tree?

Devastation In August, 1945, the United States Army dropped an atomic
bomb on Hiroshima, Japan. Many thousands perished instantaneously. Many
more thousands, poisoned by radiation, died within weeks, months, or years.
Swaths of the city were destroyed. All brush within half a mile of the epicenter
of the explosion was cleared. Bamboo trees five miles distant ignited and were
reduced to ash; no living thing within 800 yards of the blast ever grew back. But
the next spring, beside the ruins of a temple just outside the blast radius, a lone
tree sprouted from its underground roots. The *ginkgo biloba*, long cherished as a
symbol of Japan itself and as a religious symbol there, had survived.

Survivor The indomitable ginkgo is a remarkable and unusual organism. It is
remarkable in that its relatives go back 270 million years to the late Paleozoic
era. It is unusual in that it is the only remaining species of that ancient family
of trees. The ginkgo is both a living fossil and a symbol of survival. Furthermore,
it hasn't changed a whit in 1.2 million centuries. Many scientists have tried, but
thus far none have been able to explain the ginkgo's success.

City Dweller Humankind is the ginkgo's best ally. You will find ginkgo trees in
cities all across the United States because they can grow and flourish in limited
soil. Urban planners who understand the tree's accommodating attributes have
had them planted on sidewalks in great numbers. For one thing, the ginkgo
grows straight and its lowest branches rise above both pedestrians and parked
vehicles. But more important, the
ginkgo can withstand soot, auto
pollution, wide temperature swings,
whipping winds, and punishing
downpours. You'll frequently read
about powerful storms knocking
down telephone poles and toppling
massive oaks. But you'll rarely hear
about that happening to the sturdy,
resilient ginkgo.

Looking Ahead So tip your hat to
the enduring ginkgo, nature's most
persistent survivor. As our planet
warms, scientists may observe the
ginkgo to see how it fares. What do
you expect will happen?

Ginkgo leaves

Name _____ Date _____

Ancient Survivor

▶ **Answer each question. Give evidence from the essay.**

1 In line 10, the author describes the ginkgo as *indomitable*. Which word below would change the sentence's meaning if it were used in place of *indomitable*?

○ A. unconquerable   ○ B. steadfast   ○ C. tough   ○ D. frail

What evidence in the text helped you answer?

_____

_____

2 The ginkgo can *flourish* (line 17) in limited soil. In which environment would you expect cacti to *flourish*?

○ A. in a forest   ○ B. in the desert   ○ C. on grasslands   ○ D. in the tropics

What evidence in the text helped you answer? _____

_____

_____

3 What makes the title of this piece fit its subject? _____

_____

_____

4 Explain why the author asks readers to "tip your hat" (line 31) to the ginkgo. _____

_____

_____

5 Explain the author's point in calling humankind the ginkgo's "best ally" (line 16). _____

_____

_____

6 In botany, a *lobe* names a part into which a leaf divides. Look at the picture.
How can it help you explain the full name of the *ginkgo biloba*?

_____

_____

_____

Name _____ Date _____

Lessons From Superheroes

What does the author think makes superheroes truly super?

1 What do *Superman*, *Batman*, *Spider-*
2 *Man*, and *Buffy the Vampire Slayer* have
3 in common? They are all superheroes.
4 Each possesses extraordinary powers
5 that he or she uses for good purposes,
6 including fighting crime, saving
7 lives, and protecting the public from
8 super-villains. And they capture our
9 imaginations in the process. Since
10 1938, when *Superman* first appeared,
11 superheroes have dominated comic
12 books. Now they are ubiquitous in
13 movies, in plays, and on television.

14 The term *superhero* first appeared in
15 1899, but superheroes have been around
16 for centuries, battling supernatural forces
17 and using their powers to help others.
18 Our modern superheroes share traits
19 other than exceptional abilities or special
20 skills. They all have strong moral codes,
21 too. They are altruistic; they do good
22 without expecting any reward. None
23 pursues power or wealth. Some, like
24 *Superman*, act out of a sense of justice,
25 fairness, and responsibility. Others,
26 like *Buffy*, discover that they possess
27 superhuman powers, reluctantly accept
28 their destiny, and put those powers to use.

29 Most superheroes have some kind of
30 *backstory*—a life-altering experience that
31 explains how they got their powers and why
32 they employ them. That key experience may
33 be, as in *Batman's* case, a trauma. Bruce
34 Wayne, *Batman's* true identity, carries out
35 a personal vendetta after the murder of his
36 parents. He dedicates himself to fighting crime.

37 Superheroes inspire us, but not in ways you might think.
38 They do not spur us to be like we already are, only better,
39 stronger, faster. Rather, they model how to cope with adversity,
40 how to find meaning in injury or loss, and then use that
41 motivation to good purpose. We learn from them that
42 sometimes we have to grow up sooner than we'd wish to, or that
43 a stressful event can lead us to resolve to help others. For what
44 superheroes have really done for us is to tap into our capacity
45 for compassion, to understand how others feel. So it is empathy,
46 not leaping tall buildings or climbing their walls, that is a
47 genuine super power. Anyone can possess it.

Name _____ Date _____

Lessons From Superheroes

▶ **Answer each question. Give evidence from the essay.**

1 Which of the following words is a synonym for *ubiquitous* (line 12)?

○ A. ever-present   ○ B. powerful   ○ C. unusual   ○ D. lovable

What evidence in the text helped you answer? _____

_____

_____

2 Of the following activities, which is purely *altruistic* (line 21)?

○ A. selling your bicycle   ○ C. writing a thank-you note

○ B. donating to a food drive   ○ D. mowing lawns for only $5

What evidence in the text helped you answer? _____

_____

_____

3 Explain how the opening sentence of this essay is effective. _____

_____

_____

4 Why might a writer provide a character's *backstory* (line 30)? _____

_____

_____

5 Summarize the author's conclusion about the value of superheroes. _____

_____

_____

6 What makes anyone—even someone with no special power—a hero?

_____

_____

_____

_____

Name _____ Date _____

Impossible Not to Smile

How can direct quotations reveal a person's character?

1 You may have chuckled over reruns of an old TV comedy called *The Facts of*
2 *Life*, which was first broadcast in the 1980s. One of its characters, "Cousin Geri,"
3 was portrayed by actor Geri Jewell. Ms. Jewell was the first handicapped person
4 ever to play a recurring role on a prime-time television series.
5 Geri Jewell was born with a brain disorder doctors identify
6 as cerebral palsy, or CP. People with CP typically have difficulty
7 controlling their muscles, posture, and movements. Jewell's mind
8 is entirely able; it is her body, specifically the muscles needed to
9 speak clearly and move smoothly, that is a problem for her. Yet
10 she refuses to let slurred speech and a crooked walk restrict her
11 from living a full and active life.
12 Geri Jewell began performing stand-up comedy while she was
13 in college. She purposely told jokes about living with CP. Fearless
14 about speaking the truth, Geri found ways to make an awkward
15 topic far less daunting. Her humor had a distinctly gentle tone.
16 Geri Jewell has performed on television and in movies, and
17 is a motivational speaker, an active supporter for people with
18 disabilities, and a founding member of *Windmills*, a disability
19 awareness training program. What features of her personality and
20 character helped her succeed despite physical challenges? Read some
21 direct quotations from Geri Jewell to learn what makes her tick.

Cerebral means relating to the brain. *Palsy* in this case defines uncontrolled muscle movement. Cerebral palsy is not one specific disease, but a collection of physical problems that stem from abnormalities in the early development of the brain.

22 " *Questions*
23 *don't hurt.*
24 *Ignorance*
25 *does.* "

26 " *We all have*
27 *adversity so*
28 *we can grow*
29 *and evolve*
30 *and learn.* "

31 " *Smile at least twenty*
32 *times a day. Laugh*
33 *at least fifteen times*
34 *a day. Go forward in*
35 *your life and fear less.* "

36 " *My comedy is about*
37 *the human condition.*
38 *I'm trying to tell*
39 *people they should give*
40 *themselves more credit,*
41 *feel less victimized,*
42 *not be stopped by the*
43 *judgments other people*
44 *put on them.* "

45 " *Feast your eyes on*
46 *something beautiful.*
47 *You'll find it impossible*
48 *not to smile and, as a*
49 *result, will feel good*
50 *all over.* "

51 Geri Jewell subscribes to the
52 theory of the bumblebee:

53 " *Scientifically and technically,*
54 *a bumblebee's body weight*
55 *is too heavy to fly with*
56 *these tiny wings. But the*
57 *bumblebee doesn't know any*
58 *different. So [it] flies away.* "

Name _____ Date _____

Impossible Not to Smile

▶ **Answer each question. Give evidence from the biography.**

1 What is Geri Jewell's attitude about answering questions about her condition?

○ A. She doesn't mind at all if her answer might help.   ○ C. She likes questions with easy answers.

○ B. She resists talking about her physical challenges.   ○ D. She prefers not to be bothered.

How did you determine your response? _____

_____

_____

2 Which words could you substitute for *what makes her tick* (line 21) and keep the meaning the same?

○ A. what keeps her on time   ○ C. what makes her walk

○ B. why she enjoys acting   ○ D. what inspires her

What evidence in the text helped you answer? _____

_____

3 How does Geri Jewell feel about fear? _____

_____

4 What about Geri Jewell would make her an effective motivational speaker (line 17)? _____

_____

_____

5 Geri Jewell has used humor and honesty to face life head-on. Give an example of each approach.

_____

_____

_____

6 Explain how the "theory of the bumblebee" (line 52) relates to Geri Jewell's own life. _____

_____

_____

_____

_____

Name _____ Date _____

Ellis Island of the West

How can a direct quotation clarify ideas in an essay?

1   In the early part of the 20th century, most emigrants from Europe
2   seeking better lives in America entered this country at Ellis Island in
3   New York Harbor. At least those traveling in steerage did. By contrast,
4   emigrants who steamed here from Asia between 1910 and 1940 had to
5   stop first at Angel Island. There, on the largest island in San Francisco Bay,
6   they were detained, some for weeks at a time at its immigration station.
7   Others languished for months. And some people were even confined there
8   for years. As many as one million Chinese immigrants were held and
9   interrogated on Angel Island.

10   Stiff immigration laws, such as the harsh
11   Chinese Exclusion Act of 1882, made entry
12   challenging and unpleasant. Acting to
13   benefit American workers who feared that
14   the newcomers would take away jobs by
15   working for lower wages, officials made
16   it their business to try to deport as many
17   Chinese as possible. One tactic was to ask
18   the immigrants obscure questions about
19   their families or villages that they would
20   struggle to answer.

21   Men and women were housed separately
22   in barracks on Angel Island. There they
23   waited sadly and listlessly between
24   interrogations. While on the island, some
25   scrawled or scraped messages and poems
26   on barracks walls to express their anger,
27   fear, and frustration. Some of these writings
28   survive to this day.

29   A fire in 1940 destroyed the center's
30   administration building. Following
31   that, the government shut down the station and moved its work to
32   San Francisco. As on Ellis Island, a museum now inhabits the center's
33   remaining structures. It is dedicated to shedding light on the experiences of
34   those who made the long ocean journey and then suffered in confinement
35   within those walls. It also has exhibits that address the continuing story of
36   immigration.

37   Angel Island State Park is a short ferry ride from the mainland. Visitors
38   can tour the old grounds and quiet, empty buildings.

> Henry S. H. Gee, detained on Angel Island in 1940, recalls:
>
> *"My cousin and I had spent at least a year practicing for the interrogation even before we left for America. My father had written a book of questions and answers for me. There were diagrams of our village, our house. It even had a drawing of my uncle's hand and description of his moles and marks. ...We studied about an hour a day. We studied on the ship (across the Pacific Ocean) and we kept studying once we got to Angel Island, too. I was nervous."*

Name _____ Date _____

Ellis Island of the West

▶ **Answer each question. Give evidence from the essay.**

1 Which is *not* true about Angel Island?

○ A. It is now a state park.   ○ C. It was an immigration station for 30 years.

○ B. It had schools for the immigrant children.   ○ D. It is located in San Francisco Bay.

What evidence in the text helped you answer? _____

_____

_____

2 A person who *languished for months* (line 7) probably felt _____.

○ A. gloomy and sluggish   ○ C. stiff and in pain

○ B. upbeat and eager   ○ D. hopeful and expectant

What evidence in the text helped you answer? _____

_____

_____

3 How does the title of the piece fit the passage? _____

_____

4 On Angel Island, detainees were interrogated. They were asked to answer *obscure* (line 18) questions. Why did officials act in this way?

_____

_____

5 Hundreds of those who passed through Angel Island spoke or wrote about their experiences. Why might the author have chosen to include what Henry S. H. Gee remembered?

_____

_____

6 Clarify the distinction between *emigrate* and *immigrate*. Consult a dictionary, if needed. _____

_____

_____

Name _____ Date _____

Game of Change

What makes a game more than a sporting event?

1 Every early spring, as surely as the tulips burst forth,
2 *March Madness* returns. *March Madness* is the popular
3 nickname for those wild weeks each year when sports
4 fans' attention is riveted by the NCAA tournament.
5 In it, the nation's top-ranked college basketball teams
6 compete in a single-elimination tournament. From
7 it, one team emerges as national champion. But
8 something far more meaningful than a winning team
9 emerged from the competition of 1963.

10 **Match-Up** At that time, when segregation prevailed
11 in the American South, southern college basketball
12 teams were predominantly white. But the Loyola
13 University Ramblers of Chicago, which started four
14 black players, won its first-round game. Their opponent
15 in the second round would be the Maroons (now the
16 Bulldogs) of Mississippi State, an all-white squad.

17 **Resistance** Not everyone was enthusiastic about this upcoming match. In
18 fact, members of the integrated Loyola team received vicious hate mail. Still,
19 the Ramblers enjoyed the strong support of many fans around the country. On
20 the other hand, not surprisingly, many Mississippians were uncomfortable. Even
21 some players were resistant to participating in the game. The Maroons' center
22 claimed that an unwritten law forbade college teams from their state to compete
23 against black players. Furthermore, Mississippi governor Ross Barnett, an
24 acknowledged segregationist, tried to prevent the team from leaving the state.
25 His efforts at obstruction were unsuccessful; the team and its coaches secretly
26 slipped out of town. At the risk of losing his job, the college president helped in
27 the getaway.

28 **Game Night** The arena in Lansing, Michigan, was packed at game time,
29 though few Mississippi State supporters attended. Loyola won that game by 10
30 points, and then went on to capture the championship as well. But that second-
31 round game was no ordinary victory. It was "history being made," Loyola team
32 captain Jerry Harkness noted.

33 **Reconciliation** In December of 2012, the two teams played again—the first
34 time since that momentous day nearly 50 years earlier. Surviving members of
35 both ground-breaking teams were invited to attend. Those men, now in their
36 70s, were uniformly proud to have been part of that "game of change," as their
37 landmark contest has come to be known.

Name _____ Date _____

Game of Change

▶ **Answer each question. Give evidence from the essay.**

1 According to the essay, which of the following statements about the 1963 Mississippi State Maroons is true?

○ A. Their players were taller than the Loyola Ramblers were.

○ B. All the players on the team were white.

○ C. Their team captain was Jerry Harkness.

○ D. The Maroons made it to Round 3.

What evidence in the text helped you answer? _____

_____

2 In 1963, the Loyola Ramblers won the *single-elimination* (line 6) NCAA tournament. How many games did they lose?

○ A. 0   ○ B. 1   ○ C. 2   ○ D. It depended on how many teams were in the tournament.

What evidence in the text helped you answer? _____

_____

3 Why were the Mississippi State players and fans uncomfortable playing the Loyola Ramblers?

_____

4 How does the author build interest in the opening paragraph of the essay? _____

_____

_____

5 What do the actions of the 1963 president of Mississippi State reveal about his character? Explain.

_____

_____

6 Based on your reading of this essay, explain its title. Summarize the change that took place.

_____

_____

_____

_____

Name _____ Date _____

Preserving Audio Archives

Why do cultures wish to preserve important artifacts?

1   Welcome, young librarians, researchers, music lovers, and historians. Let
2   me begin with a question. *Where can you go to listen to the world's largest public*
3   *collection of sound recordings?* [pause] You can visit my workplace. I'm referring to
4   the Library of Congress in our nation's capital. Founded in 1800, it is our oldest
5   federal cultural institution.
6   Listening to some 3.5 million recordings that represent 110 years of sound
7   recording history is easy. All you need is a Public Reader Registration Card. This
8   card is free to anyone doing library research there.
9   The vast collection covers a wide range of subjects and formats. It contains
10 more than 500,000 LPs, 450,000 78-rpm discs and 150,000 45-rpm discs, over
11 500,000 unpublished discs, 200,000 CDs, 175,000 tape reels, and 75,000 audio
12 cassettes. The emphasis is on sound recordings produced here in the United
13 States. You future scholars should know that the collection's curators focus
14 on acquiring recordings of historical significance. They pay little attention to
15 contemporary views of their popularity or aesthetic value.
16   You can listen to live musical performances, historic speeches, interviews,
17 radio broadcasts, and authors reading their own works. You music fans will be
18 glad to know that most genres are represented here, with particular strength in
19 opera, chamber music, folk, jazz, musical theater, and classical music. Nearly
20 every sound recording format is represented. We have wire recordings, wax
21 cylinders, piano rolls, vinyl records, MIDI files, and even music box discs.
22   The Library of Congress is always looking to acquire new items and to figure
23 out how to preserve them. Although we have been able to record sound for
24 125 years now, many recordings
25 are in poor shape. And some recent
26 recordings are in danger because
27 rapid changes in technology have
28 rendered their software obsolete. With
29 such issues in mind, we have recently
30 unveiled a National Recording
31 Preservation Plan to protect and
32 perpetuate our country's precious
33 audio archives. We hope to transform
34 the way we preserve sound and
35 maintain this national treasure. We
36 hope that you are as excited about it
37 as we are.
38   Please come visit us. We're located
39 right behind the Capitol Building.
40 Thank you very much.

Early wax cylinder recordings
and the type of machine used
to play them

Name _____ Date _____

Preserving Audio Archives

▶ **Answer each question. Give evidence from the speech.**

1 Which is *not* an example of a sound recording format?

○ A. MIDI file   ○ B. 45-rpm disc   ○ C. wax cylinder   ○ D. piece of sheet music

What evidence in the text helped you answer? _____

_____

_____

2 Which of the following inventions has been *rendered obsolete* (line 28)?

○ A. the automobile   ○ B. the paper clip   ○ C. the telegraph   ○ D. eyeglasses

What evidence in the text helped you answer? _____

_____

_____

3 What job do *curators* (line 13) have in a library or museum, and what is the particular focus of the curators of the audio archives of the Library of Congress?

_____

_____

4 Who is the intended audience for this speech? Explain. _____

_____

_____

5 Why does the speaker call the collected sound recordings a "national treasure" (line 35)? Explain.

_____

_____

_____

6 Based on the speech, what is the purpose of preserving audio archives? _____

_____

_____

Name _____ Date _____

The Sky's the Limit

How does this essay reflect the idea of rising from the ashes?

1 **Fire!** On October 8, 1871, a fire started in a wooden barn behind Patrick and
2 Catherine O'Leary's house. Legend holds that their cow was at fault: It had
3 knocked over a lit lantern. It had been a dry summer in Chicago; the ground
4 was parched and the blaze spread briskly. By the time the fire exhausted
5 itself two days later, it left behind a 3.3-square-mile barren swath through the
6 heart of the city. But as it happens, the simultaneous emergence of two major
7 innovations turned that disaster into a significant milestone in Chicago's
8 history. For around the same time that a new kind of construction was being
9 invented, so, too, were electric-powered elevators.

10 **Innovation** Large structures at that time relied fully on stone and brick,
11 which limited how high they could rise. Then, in 1885, architect William Jenney
12 completed the 10-story Home Insurance Building atop downtown Chicago's
13 rubble. Jenney's unique building was innovative because it employed steel
14 frames that completely supported its walls, making it sturdy and fireproof. And
15 since having supporting walls was no longer necessary, buildings like this could
16 have as many large windows as the architects desired. *Steel-beam construction*, a
17 new form of architecture, rose above the ashes of the devastating fire.

18 **Ascent** But you can't have skyscrapers without
19 elevators. Although the Otis Company had
20 been manufacturing elevators since the 1840s,
21 they were steam-powered, painfully slow, and
22 frequently unsafe. In 1880 in Germany, Werner
23 von Siemens invented the first electrically
24 powered one. A few years after that, William
25 Sprague significantly improved the electric
26 elevator's speed and safety. Now the sky was
27 the limit, and hundred-story buildings were no
28 longer pipe dreams.

29 **Results** America's architectural giants—
30 Daniel Burnham and Louis Sullivan among
31 them—flocked to Illinois to exhibit their
32 talents. Within a few years, they and others
33 had changed the city's skyline. To this day,
34 Chicago is considered a marvel of architecture
35 and design. In a way, it all started with the
36 O'Learys, or maybe with their cow.

Jenney's building was supported by
a steel skeleton of vertical columns
and horizontal beams.

Name _____ Date _____

The Sky's the Limit

▶ **Answer each question. Give evidence from the essay.**

1 When two events are *simultaneous* (line 6), they happen _____.

○ A. slowly   ○ B. in the same place   ○ C. at the same time   ○ D. separately

What evidence in the text helped you answer? _____

_____

_____

2 What was innovative about William Jenney's 1885 building?

○ A. It offered great views of the city.   ○ C. It was located where a fire had burned.

○ B. It housed an insurance company.   ○ D. It was constructed with steel frames.

What evidence in the text helped you answer? _____

_____

_____

3 How are Otis, Siemens, and Sprague connected? Explain. _____

_____

_____

4 What does *changed the city's skyline* (line 33) mean? _____

_____

_____

5 Why did the terrible Chicago fire of 1871 get the attention of the nation's top architects?

_____

_____

6 Summarize the cause-and-effect relationship between the fire in the barn and the change in the Chicago skyline.

_____

_____

_____

_____

Name _____ Date _____

Not Rocket Science

How did an accident lead to a modern technology?

1   When we envision rockets, we imagine mighty missiles that can reach
2   soaring heights at dazzling speeds. Yet the roots of modern rocketry lie in
3   experiments of the past. Ingenuity and bold thinking have taken us from
4   primitive exploding devices to vehicles that can travel deep into outer space.
5   It is unclear when the first true rockets appeared, though new research
6   suggests that rocketry was invented by puzzled but fearless Chinese alchemists.
7   *Alchemists* were the chemists of the middle ages. Their work mixed science,
8   magic, and philosophy.

9   **Earliest Attempts** In about 400 B.C., a Greek scientist built one of the first
10 devices to successfully use some principles of rocket flight. He captured steam
11 to propel a wooden pigeon that hung from a wire. People were amused and
12 impressed by the show. But this wooden bird was not a true rocket.

13 **First Use** True rockets operate solely by combustion and self-propulsion.
14 The first reported use of true rockets came in 1232 when the Chinese fought
15 off Mongol invaders with "flying fire lances." Although it's unknown how
16 effective these weapons were, one can certainly imagine that they terrified
17 the bewildered enemy. But these rough devices did not appear out of the blue.
18 They were centuries in the making.

19 **Fumbling Toward Success** Seeking a formula
20 for immortality, ninth century Chinese alchemists
21 began to haphazardly mix ingredients and
22 observe the results. Eventually, their fumbling led
23 to a crude formula—not for everlasting life, but
24 for gunpowder! Over the years, those adventurous
25 early tinkerers refined the recipe by trial and error
26 (and several burnt beards). They filled bamboo
27 tubes with a mixture of saltpeter, sulfur, and
28 charcoal dust. Then they tossed them into a fire
29 and watched "ground rats" shoot about the floor
30 in all directions. During one such demonstration
31 at a banquet, an empress was petrified as the
32 rockets skittered under her chair.

33 They didn't do it deliberately, but the Chinese
34 had stumbled upon the property of self-
35 propulsion. They had accidentally fashioned the
36 first true rockets.

Name _____ Date _____

Not Rocket Science

▷ **Answer each question. Give evidence from the essay.**

1 What two features define a true rocket?

○ A. speed and flight   ○ C. propulsion and alchemy

○ B. combustion and self-propulsion   ○ D. bamboo and saltpeter

What evidence in the text helped you answer? _____

_____

_____

2 Which of the following words could you substitute for *Ingenuity* in line 3 without changing the meaning of the sentence?

○ A. Philosophy   ○ B. Bewilderment   ○ C. Inventiveness   ○ D. Sophistication

What evidence in the text helped you answer?

_____

_____

3 How did Chinese alchemists accidentally invent a true rocket? _____

_____

_____

4 Identify two clues in the text that help you determine the meaning of *immortality* (line 20).

_____

_____

_____

5 Why might the author have presented "flying fire lances" (line 15) and "ground rats" (line 29) inside quotation marks?

_____

_____

6 How would you explain the title the author chose for this essay? _____

_____

_____

Name _____ Date _____

Surprises in Ice

How might searching for answers raise entirely new questions?

1   Methane is a potent greenhouse gas that is
2 implicated in climate change. Methane is a product
3 of emissions from landfills, large-scale ranches,
4 land-clearing fires, and natural gas pipeline leaks.
5 The United States alone generates about 36 million
6 tons of methane gas per year.

7 **New Discovery** Until recently, scientists believed
8 that the earth's atmosphere was untainted by
9 humans prior to the Industrial Revolution.
10 Now, thanks to recent discoveries made within
11 Greenland's pristine deep ice sheet, they know better.
12   A team of American and European scientists
13 probed deep within the layers of that ice. They
14 knew that methane gas production occurred
15 naturally in the atmosphere, but in low
16 concentrations. But they wanted to find out if there was a relationship between
17 warmer climate periods and increased methane gas levels. So they analyzed
18 minute ice bubbles going back 2,000 years and made a key discovery. They found
19 that methane concentrations did indeed rise and fall over time, but not in step
20 with changes in temperatures. This was surprising. The researchers surmised that
21 the changes in methane gas levels must have been caused by something else.

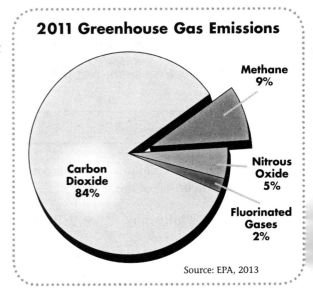

2011 Greenhouse Gas Emissions

Methane
9%

Nitrous
Oxide
5%

Carbon
Dioxide
84%

Fluorinated
Gases
2%

Source: EPA, 2013

22 **Cause and Effect** That "something" turned out to be human activity.
23 Specifically, it was the growth in farming and industry. The scientists spotted a
24 rise in atmospheric methane gas at the same time as large-scale agriculture and
25 metallurgy began in Rome and China. In ancient Rome, domesticated cows and
26 sheep excreted methane gas as a product of digestion. In China, the expansion of
27 rice fields also produced the gas. And in both empires, blacksmiths were burning
28 large amounts of wood as part of the process of forming metal weapons. This, too,
29 increased the amounts of methane.
30   The scientists also discovered that when civilizations declined and their industry
31 and activity decreased, methane emissions dropped. On the other hand, they
32 found that as human population rose significantly over the centuries, the amount
33 of methane gas in the air did, too. That increase in methane went hand in hand
34 with upticks in trade, agriculture, and manufacturing.

35 **Looking Ahead** The exciting discovery that humans were altering the
36 atmosphere long before the 18th and 19th centuries encourages scientists to explore
37 further. They are looking back to find atmospheric methane amounts *before* human
38 activity. It may change the way they look ahead, too. Scientists hope to clarify the
39 connection between current and future methane emissions and climate change.

Name _____ Date _____

Surprises in Ice

▶ **Answer each question. Give evidence from the article.**

1 The article states that methane gas is *implicated* (line 2) in climate change. Which of the following is an antonym for *implicated*?

○ A. associated   ○ B. connected   ○ C. involved   ○ D. cleared

What evidence in the text helped you answer? _____

_____

_____

2 According to the graph, about what portion of the total greenhouse gas emissions in 2011 was methane?

○ A. about nine-tenths   ○ B. about four-fifths   ○ C. about one-tenth   ○ D. about a fourth

What evidence in the text helped you answer? _____

_____

3 What big discovery surprised scientists when they studied the Greenland ice samples? _____

_____

_____

4 Based on the recent discoveries, what do scientists now believe causes changes in methane gas levels in the atmosphere?

_____

_____

5 Why does the author refer to the 18th and 19th centuries in the final paragraph? _____

_____

_____

6 Many articles include statements that prompt new questions. What might you ask about the amount of methane gas the United States generates in a year?

_____

_____

_____

Name _____ Date _____

Astronomers' Desert

How can a barren and remote location have great value?

1 **A Desert's Desert** The Atacama Desert stretches about 600 miles from Peru's
2 southern border into northern Chile. Consisting primarily of lifeless salt basins
3 and sand, this cool, arid region is one of the driest places in the world. It gets
4 less than half an inch of rain in 100 years. It is so dry there that surrounding
5 mountains soaring more than 22,000 feet into the sky have no glaciers. The
6 soil is so like that of Mars that NASA engineers have used the area to test
7 equipment. And because the landscape resembles the surface of the Red Planet,
8 some science fiction shows with scenes on Mars have been filmed there.

9 **Uninhabitable...** The Atacama has an area that is approximately the size of
10 Cuba. It contains some truly sterile, intimidating stretches where rain has never
11 been recorded. There's no grass, no trees or bushes, no cacti or lizards, not even a
12 gnat. It's remote, cold, and empty. The people who inhabit northern Chile don't
13 live there. They reside along the coast, in oasis towns, or in the few remaining
14 copper or sodium nitrate mining camps.

15 **...But Heavenly** But the Atacama is the perfect home for one thing. It's the
16 ideal spot for teams of scientists to conduct astronomical observations. The high
17 altitude, the nearly nonexistent cloud cover, the dry, thin air, and the lack of
18 light pollution make it an optimal location for telescopes.

19 **ALMA** The latest and greatest telescope has just made its appearance. Set on a
20 high Atacama plateau, the $1.3 billion ALMA is the largest radio telescope ever
21 built. It will allow astronomers to hunt for information about the origin of the
22 universe and to investigate phenomena like black holes and the Big Bang. It will
23 enable them to spy into the most distant, dark corners of the universe. Things
24 that were invisible will be so no longer.

25 **Looking Ahead** Delighted astronomers have already made some fascinating
26 discoveries. For instance, they have now gotten an astonishing look at a system
27 of planets orbiting a star 25 light years away. In addition, they've gathered
28 key data about origins of life. This
29 happened when they detected an
30 essential biochemical building block
31 in gases that surround another star.
32 That one is 400 light years distant,
33 and very much like our sun. How
34 ironic that one of the most barren
35 places on earth will likely harvest a
36 wealth of far-reaching scientific data!
37 The whole world is waiting to see.

The ALMA telescope consists of an array of antennae.

Name _____ Date _____

Astronomers' Desert

▶ **Answer each question. Give evidence from the article.**

1 What must visitors to the Atacama bring to its *arid* (line 3) climate?

　○ A. books to read　　○ B. sturdy shoes　　○ C. telescopes　　○ D. drinking water

What evidence in the text helped you answer? _____

_____

_____

2 Which of the following might you find in the Atacama?

　○ A. an abandoned mine　　○ B. a cattle ranch　　○ C. palm trees　　○ D. camels

What evidence in the text helped you answer? _____

_____

_____

3 Why do astronomers find the Atacama so welcoming for their work? _____

_____

_____

4 Why would the high mountains around the Atacama lack glaciers (lines 4 and 5)? _____

_____

_____

5 What is it about the ALMA telescope that has made astronomers so delighted? _____

_____

_____

6 Discuss the role of geography in the science of astronomy. _____

_____

_____

_____

_____

Name _____ Date _____

The Great Wall of Los Angeles

How does this essay link visual art, location, and community?

1 *I want to produce art that has meaning beyond simple decorative*
2 *value. I hope to use public space to create public voice and*
3 *consciousness about the presence of people who are often the majority*
4 *of the population but who may not be represented in any visual way.*

5 These are the words of Judith Baca. She is an artist, educator, activist,
6 and community arts pioneer. Born and raised in Los Angeles, Baca is the
7 inspiration and force behind one of that city's true cultural landmarks.
8 Her creation is the *Great Wall of Los Angeles*. This is a half-mile pictorial
9 representation of the history of ethnic peoples in California. This
10 enormous mural depicts scenes from prehistoric times through the 1950s.
11 It is one of America's most respected monuments to interracial harmony.
12 The Great Wall was the first public art project of the Social and Public
13 Art Resource Center (SPARC). The project began in 1974 and took five
14 summers. Baca planned and painted alongside more than 400 young
15 muralists and their families. Under her guidance and supervision, they
16 created the wall, one panel at a time, along a flood channel in the San
17 Fernando Valley. The young artists tackled such periods as the coming
18 of the Spanish, Chinese immigration, the Depression, the arrival of
19 dustbowl refugees, world wars, and the birth of rock and roll. In the
20 words of Judy Baca, "Perhaps most overwhelming to me about [this]
21 experience has been learning of the courage of individuals who endured,
22 spoke out, and overcame seemingly insurmountable obstacles. It was
23 true both of the people we painted and of ourselves, the Mural Makers."
24 In 2011, the wall was
25 splendidly restored. It had
26 suffered damage from
27 flooding, air pollution,
28 heat, and exposure to
29 direct sunlight. And now,
30 with a new grant from The
31 National Endowment for
32 the Arts, work on the wall
33 goes forward again. Judy
34 Baca wants it "…to bring
35 the past into the present to
36 inspire the future."

Name _____ Date _____

The Great Wall of Los Angeles

▶ **Answer each question. Give evidence from the essay.**

1 Which description best depicts who Judith Baca is?

○ A. She restores decorative art projects.

○ B. She is an involved artist, teacher, and community leader.

○ C. She is an artist born, raised, and living in Los Angeles.

○ D. She is an outspoken California historian.

What evidence in the text helped you answer? _____

_____

_____

2 What is true about the kind of art Judith Baca seeks to produce?

○ A. She prefers outdoor works near water.

○ B. She favors art that focuses on the present.

○ C. She makes art that speaks to and for all people.

○ D. She prefers to work independently of others.

What evidence in the text helped you answer? _____

_____

3 Find the word *insurmountable* in line 22. Describe how to use word-study skills to unlock its meaning. Then suggest a synonym.

_____

_____

4 What makes the *Great Wall of Los Angeles* one of the city's "cultural landmarks" (line 7)? _____

_____

_____

5 What reasons would you suggest for why it took so long to complete the *Great Wall of Los Angeles*?

_____

_____

_____

6 Look closely at the photograph. How does it add to your understanding of the mural? _____

_____

_____

Name _____ Date _____

Bad Burger

What elements in this e-mail letter make it effective?

1 From: Julia Kidd<JKidd@ZTL.net>
2 Sent: Wednesday, June 1, 2014, 01:13 PM
3 To: Best Burgers<BestBurgers@sync.net>

4 Subject: Customer Complaint

5 Dear Best Burgers Manager,
6   I am the kind of customer your restaurant—or any restaurant—would relish.
7 I not only adore your food and appreciate your establishment's atmosphere
8 and the staff's courteous and accommodating service, I return again and again
9 with a smile and a hearty appetite. Furthermore, I rave to everyone I know
10 about the entire experience. In particular, I mention the delectable Best Burgers
11 Special, which, to me, is heaven on a bun. But when I dined last night at your
12 place, planning to impress my out-of-town friends, I received an unwelcome and
13 embarrassing surprise.
14   Frankly, the Best Burgers food was not up to your usual rigorous standards.
15 Our burgers were uniformly over-cooked and practically unpalatable. The
16 cheese toppings were so meagerly applied to be barely detectable, and the
17 sweet potato fries and stuffed mushrooms were loaded with grease and absent
18 their customary flavor. In addition, our desserts (which I normally savor!)
19 were a dreary disappointment. The apple cobbler was soggy and tasteless, the
20 cheesecake dry, and the coffee oily and lukewarm. Imagine my unhappiness
21 and humiliation! To make matters worse, Anita, the world's greatest server, was
22 nowhere to be seen.
23   My friends were clearly underwhelmed by their dining experience; my
24 reputation as a reliable foodie has been sadly diminished.
25   What has happened? Have you changed chefs or recipes? Are you now
26 purchasing meat from another distributor, using different kinds of potatoes,
27 trying out new cooking oils, or breaking in new kitchen equipment? Whatever
28 the reason, I find myself in a quandary. Should I return? And if I do, what
29 should I expect when I settle into a booth and dive into my meal?
30   I'm not ordinarily a complainer, and I realize that Anita is entitled to a night
31 off! But I've so enjoyed your restaurant that I hope, with all due respect, that
32 my letter alerts you to problems that I, and perhaps others, have unhappily
33 encountered.
34   Sincerely yours,
35   Julia Kidd

Name _____ Date _____

Bad Burger

▶ **Answer each question. Give evidence from the e-mail.**

1 Why does the writer return to Best Burgers so often?

○ A. The restaurant has low prices and huge portions.

○ B. She likes the food, the atmosphere, and the service.

○ C. Best Burgers is located very close to where she lives.

○ D. Best Burgers updates its kitchen equipment all the time.

What evidence in the text helped you answer? _____

_____

2 Which type of food would most people agree is *unpalatable* (line 15)?

○ A. pancakes burnt to a crisp   ○ C. food that was defrosted

○ B. homemade applesauce   ○ D. food made with natural ingredients

What evidence in the text helped you answer? _____

_____

3 What does the word *quandary* (line 28) mean? Why is Julia in a quandary? _____

_____

_____

4 Why did Julia feel a sense of humiliation (line 21)? _____

_____

_____

5 Analyze the technique the writer uses to begin her letter of complaint. Why take that approach?

_____

_____

_____

6 How would you describe the tone of this letter? _____

_____

_____

Name _____ Date _____

Off-Leash

What information does the writer give to make her point?

1 To the Editor:
2   In our congested city, my
3 Chella, like all dogs, is allowed
4 outside only when on leash.
5 She must be on a leash when
6 strolling the sidewalks, crossing
7 the streets, entering stores that
8 graciously permit her, and even
9 while frolicking in our spacious
10 parks. This is a completely
11 understandable rule in a city
12 chock-a-block with pooches.
13 It's best for the safety of others
14 and of the dogs themselves.
15 Thankfully, there is a time each
16 day when dogs are allowed to
17 be off-leash in some city parks.
18 That's a wonderful regulation
19 since dogs are meant to run
20 free when they can, to be their
21 natural curious, playful selves
22 without hindrance. It is with the
23 allotted leash-free times that I
24 take issue.
25   Where we live, that time
26 period is from 9 P.M. to 9 A.M.
27 The nighttime hours are
28 sensible, but few care to amble
29 into our park in darkness. It's
30 the early morning time that's
31 problematic, for that's when the
32 park hosts races. Particularly
33 on weekends, the park roads
34 are clogged with competitive
35 runners, marathon walkers, and
36 whirring packs of cyclists. This
37 is unfortunate because this is
38 when many dog owners have
39 their sole opportunity to provide
40 their dogs off-leash freedom.
41   Pairing hundreds of free-
42 roaming dogs with these

43 athletes is unfair to dogs and
44 racers alike. At best, dogs must
45 wait for long periods just to
46 cross the roads as the racers
47 pass. At worst, a perky pup
48 could easily romp into a pack
49 of runners or cyclists and cause
50 serious accidents. I myself have
51 seen this happen.
52   What to do? I fully
53 understand the value of
54 holding these races, many of
55 which are for good causes.
56 And I appreciate that it is
57 preferable to schedule them
58 early in the day when parks
59 are less jammed with people
60 and, during summer months,
61 when temperatures are more
62 cooperative. Therefore, I don't
63 suggest changing the race times
64 to accommodate the dog owners
65 and dogs. But I do propose
66 extending the off-leash hours
67 to 11 A.M. In accordance with
68 the change, I think posting
69 dates for planned races both
70 online and on signs placed
71 at park entrances would be a
72 useful step.
73   I adore seeing Chella prance
74 about with a prized stick in her
75 mouth, chase another pooch
76 around a tree, or sprint after
77 a thrown ball. But I prefer
78 seeing these things under safer
79 conditions. I fully support a
80 sensible change in off-leash
81 times.

82 —Madison Rosen

Name _____ Date _____

Off-Leash

▶ **Answer each question. Give evidence from the letter.**

1 What does the letter writer *not* do in arguing for changing leash laws?

○ A. She presents both sides of the argument.   ○ C. She offers a possible solution.

○ B. She expresses anger and frustration.   ○ D. She supports her position.

What evidence in the text helped you answer? _____

_____

_____

2 What makes a city *congested* (line 2)?

○ A. The air quality and visibility are poor.

○ B. There are many restaurants and food carts.

○ C. It has few parks, playgrounds, or open spaces.

○ D. It has crowded streets, sidewalks, and public areas.

What evidence in the text helped you answer? _____

_____

3 Explain what it means for dogs to run *without hindrance* (line 22). _____

_____

_____

4 Why do you think the writer used the word *whirring* (line 36) to describe packs of racing cyclists?

_____

_____

5 How would you describe the tone of Madison Rosen's letter to the editor? _____

_____

_____

6 Why would the writer present her opinion as a letter to the editor of a newspaper? _____

_____

_____

_____

Name _____ Date _____

Table Tennis

What different kinds of data and information does the author present?

1   Table tennis is a game for two (singles) or four (doubles) players. Players
2   use racquets called *paddles* to hit a small, light ball back and forth across a
3   table divided by a low net. The object of the game is to win points by making
4   shots opponents are unable to return.

5   **The table** is 2.74 m long, 1.52 m wide, and must lie horizontal to the floor
6   76 cm above it. The table, generally made of wood, is divided at the midpoint
7   of its length by a net. But any material will do as long as a ball dropped from
8   30 cm gives a bounce of about 23 cm. The playing surface must be dark-
9   colored with 2-cm white marking lines around its perimeter. For doubles, the
10   playing surface needs a 3-mm line dividing its length into halves.

11   **The net** is a strip of mesh 1.83 m long and 15.25 cm high. It is suspended
12   across the center of the table by a cord fastened to posts at either side of
13   the table.

14   **The playing area** is required to be a minimum of 5.5 m from either
15   end and 2.75 m from either side. The minimum height is 3.5 m. These
16   measurements are defined only for international play.

17   **The racquet** may have any size, shape, or mass for its handle. However,
18   its blade must be of a uniform dark color. It has to be covered with a plain,
19   pimpled rubber not exceeding 2 mm in thickness. The surface not used for
20   hitting is exempted from this covering rule.

21   **The ball** must be white or orange, have a diameter of 40 mm, and weigh
22   2.7 g. It is made of celluloid or a similar plastic.

23   **Game and Match** The
24   player or pair that scores 21
25   points first wins unless both
26   have scored 20 points. In
27   the latter case, the winner
28   is the first to score two more
29   points than the opposition.
30   A match consists either of
31   the best of three games or
32   the best of five games.

Name _____ Date _____

Table Tennis

▶ **Answer each question. Give evidence from the game guide.**

1 What is the proper name for the part of the racquet with which players hit the ball?

○ A. post   ○ B. paddle   ○ C. handle   ○ D. blade

What evidence in the text helped you answer? _____

_____

_____

2 Which is a reasonable estimate of the area of an official table?

○ A. about 1 square meter   ○ C. between 3 and 5 square meters

○ B. between 1 and 3 square meters   ○ D. greater than 6 square meters

What evidence in the text helped you answer? _____

_____

_____

3 Why do the rules state that the table surface must be dark-colored (lines 8 and 9)? _____

_____

_____

4 In an official game of table tennis, can a game end with a score of 25 to 24? Explain. _____

_____

_____

5 Who might be the audience for this type of writing? _____

_____

_____

6 Review the information the guide provides. What rules for playing a game of table tennis are *not* stated?

_____

_____

_____

Literature Passages

Passage 1: Gym Jam

1. D; Sample answer: I read each choice and then reread paragraph 2. It mentions the ideas in choices A, B, and C, so I picked D (lines 15–19). **2.** B; Sample answer: Mikayla had a lot of things to deal with as a new kid in a new school in a new city and it was exhausting (lines 1–14). Her head probably felt like it was spinning from all the new information. **3.** Sample answer: Mikayla loves to sing, and does so every chance she gets (lines 20–22). **4.** Sample answer: Kevin's invitation spoke to her love of singing and was a chance to get to know some of her schoolmates better (lines 20–23, 28–35). **5.** Sample answer: She felt cheered up by a chance to sing with others, by being invited to be part of a group, and by having something fun to look forward to (lines 36–41). **6.** Sample answer: Kevin invited Mikayla to the Gym Jam. She linked *gym* with athletics or sports. She missed the word *jam* or didn't know its musical connection (lines 25–28).

Passage 2: The Golden Axe

1. C; Sample answer: I picked C because the woodcutter knew he couldn't swim or dive in such *depths* (lines 10–12), and Mercury plunged *deep* into the pool (line 16). **2.** A; Sample answer: The only woodcutter who was honest was the first one. He not only got his axe back (lines 24–26), but was rewarded as well (lines 27–30). Those who lied were punished (lines 36–40). **3.** Sample answer: The woodcutter used it every day for his work (lines 1–2), and didn't have the money to be able to replace it (lines 8–10). **4.** Sample answer: The woodcutter was embarrassed having to explain to a god that he lost his axe because it flew out of his hands and that he was too poor to get a new one (lines 8–15). **5.** Sample answer: Mercury was caring and helpful (lines 16–30), but didn't tolerate lying or trickery (lines 38–40). **6.** Sample answer: A fable is a short and simple story, often with talking animals or gods. It is written to teach a useful life lesson.

Passage 3: Sounds of Spring

1. D; Sample answer: It sounds like the mitt is experienced, has caught a lot of pitches (lines 10–14), and has been through spring training and baseball seasons before (lines 34–36). **2.** C; Sample answer: I know that a *heater* is some kind of pitch, and because the writer contrasts the 95-mph pitch with a 75-mph pitch (lines 32–33), I picked C. **3.** Sample answer: The monologue is given by a catcher's mitt (line 9), so the *I* throughout the piece is the mitt. **4.** Sample answer: I know that the glove gets tossed into a locker (line 35), so the metal cell is a description of the locker from the glove's point of view. **5.** Sample answer: The glove is funny (lines 7–9, 19–20, 39–41), self-important (lines 10–11), opinionated (lines 25–26), knowledgeable about baseball (lines 10–17, 30–32), and whiny (line 21). **6.** Sample answer: First, a glove cannot really talk, so that's a funny and absurd idea to begin with (line 9). The writer uses surprise (lines 7–9), exaggeration (lines 19–20, 22–24, 27–28), a comic discussion among gloves (lines 24–25), and plays with the idea that a catcher's mitt has ideas, opinions, and feelings!

Passage 4: What Goes Around...

1. B; Sample answer: In lines 4 and 5, it says that the man divided his wealth into equitable portions. Then in line 8 it says that the portions were identical. So, he divided his wealth equally and fairly. *Even-handed*, *equivalent*, and *just* all seem to describe this. The opposite is *dissimilar*. **2.** A; Sample answer: When the old man noticed that his daughters stopped caring for him once they learned about their inheritance, he began to question whether they ever really loved him (lines 10–18). **3.** Sample answer: He asks his daughters to help comfort him in his final days (lines 6–7). **4.** Sample answer: Once they knew they would get big inheritances, they stopped trying so hard to be nice to their father (lines 10–13). **5.** Sample answer: The daughters assumed that the trunks would be full of even more money for them to inherit, so they became helpful again so they could get some of it (lines 33–37). **6.** Sample answer: To reward his daughters for being kind and taking care of him, the father was going to repay them with his generosity (lines 3–7). But when they turned against him, they lost his respect and got no more from him (lines 9–18, 33–40).

Passage 5: City in the Sky

1. C; Sample answer: I read, "This site has been continually inhabited for more than nine centuries" (lines 12–14). **2.** D; Sample answer: "Land of enchantment" sounds like a nickname (line 8). **3.** Sample answer: The author uses a word that suggests that the walk was difficult and that he or she was reluctant to walk up in the first place, since they could have taken the bus (lines 22–26). **4.** Sample answer: It is probably hard to live in a place where you have to climb up and down the high mesa all the time and live without electricity or running water (lines 10–12, 22–26, 31–32). **5.** Sample answer: The mission is the most prominent structure on the mesa (lines 34–35). Leroy's father's job as a caretaker is a highly respected one (lines 37–38). **6.** Sample answer: I think it means that they traveled a long way to New Mexico from a different time zone, and had a guide book, which tells me they didn't know the area (lines 6–8, 39–41).

Passage 6: Thief of Fire

1. B; Sample answer: Prometheus was proud to have created the mortals (lines 2–5); he hoped to teach them about civilization (lines 10–11); and he felt generous toward them (lines 12–21). **2.** C; Sample answer: Zeus ordered the mortals to do this to show their obedience to him (lines 13–15). **3.** Sample answer: *Defiance* means disobeying orders on purpose (lines 12–13). Prometheus knew Zeus would be angry if he didn't follow his commands, but he didn't care (lines 18–23). A similar word is *rebellion*. **4.** Sample answer: Line 1 says that he was immortal—which means able to live forever. **5.** Sample answer: Zeus was the most powerful god of all (lines 1–2). He ordered other gods around (lines 2–4, 8–9); he had a wicked temper (lines 17, 21–23); and he didn't hesitate to take revenge (lines 24–39). **6.** Sample answer: Those dots mean that there is more to come, or that the story isn't over. It makes me want to know about Pandora to see how Zeus continues punishing mortals.

Passage 7: Out Back of Beyond

1. B; Sample answer: I reread the beginning to notice the very first time Liza felt uncomfortable (lines 15–17). **2.** D; Sample answer: I picked D because the other three choices are reasonable synonyms for *excursion,* which means some kind of outing or trip, since they are going on a hike (lines 1–2). **3.** Sample answer: The footprints were surprisingly big and deep, which suggests that a huge creature made them—and might be nearby to attack the hikers (lines 26–28). **4.** Sample answer: Tito seems to be curious (lines 24–26), he doubts there is such a thing as Sasquatch (line 24), he is fearless and keeps his cool (lines 29–34), but knows when to leave (lines 38–39). **5.** Sample answer: The text says that they were out on a "hike on a little-used trail" (line 2). "Out Back of Beyond" sounds like somewhere past where you ought to be, or somewhere beyond where things are normal, or as they should be. **6.** Sample answer: In line 23, it says that Sasquatch ran away from the hikers, and in lines 37 and 38 that Sasquatch howled. That makes me think that Sasquatch was probably as afraid of the hikers as they were of it.

Passage 8: Dogs and a Dinghy

1. B; Sample answer: I reread the last paragraph, which spells out the problem clearly (lines 33–39). **2.** A; Sample answer: First I figured out that *extraneous* means *extra* or *unneeded* (lines 3–5). Then I read each choice to see which was not important to solving Willa's problem. I picked A, because B, C, and D all matter (lines 16–32). **3.** Sample answer: Mollie and Pastrami can't be left alone together, and neither can Teddy and Mollie (lines 23–32). **4.** Sample answer: She can leave Teddy and Pastrami alone together (lines 23–31). **5.** Sample answer: I think the author means that the solution can be clever, simple, precise, and clear—once you figure it out. **6.** Sample answer: First, Willa can row Mollie across, leave her, and then row back. Next, she can bring Pastrami across and leave him there, but bring Mollie back and leave her on the near bank. Finally, she can take Teddy across, leave him with Pastrami, and row back for Mollie (lines 21–32).

Passage 9: Ship's Boy

1. A; Sample answer: First I figured out that *menial* means not that important or skilled because it describes one of Juan's tasks as being essential (lines 7–9). I read all four choices and doing laundry didn't seem like it needed that much skill to do.

2. B; Sample answer: The author uses the words *frigid* (line 26), *gloomy* and *awesome* (line 28), and *majestic* and *terrifying* (line 33), so I picked the choice most like those descriptions. **3.** Sample answer: Storms tossed the ships around like toys (line 13); they didn't really know where they were going or whether they'd ever get there (lines 5–6, 18–24); they were at sea for long stretches (lines 24–27); and there were strong currents, fierce winds, and violent gales (lines 33–35). **4.** Sample answer: They were going to a place no one had ever been before, so I think *uncharted* means not on any maps or sea charts (lines 5–6, 18–24). **5.** Sample answer: His job was to turn the sand clocks (lines 7–9). So, he was responsible for keeping time for the whole ship, which would have been an important, serious, and necessary task. **6.** Sample answer: It takes place in the past (lines 3, 25) and is based on real events, places, things, and people. The fiction part is that Juan is a character the author made up to describe an adventure that really happened.

Informational Text Passages

Passage 10: Private Eye

1. D; Sample answer: The author says that the term comes from America (line 19). **2.** B; Sample answer: In lines 35 and 36, it says that the façade displayed the company's logo. A sign like that is usually on the outside, on the front of a building. **3.** Sample answer: *Mug shot* sounds like it's a slang term, and the author also wanted to call attention to it and its link to Pinkerton (lines 24–26). **4.** Sample answer: The author says that Pinkerton's greatest fame came when he ruined a plot to assassinate Abraham Lincoln (lines 27–29). **5.** Sample answer: A one-sentence paragraph makes the question stand out, which shows that answering this question is the main purpose of this article. **6.** Sample answer: The slogan suggests that the investigators who worked for Pinkerton would always keep their eyes open, stay alert, and not miss things while doing their job.

Passage 11: A Writer's Story

1. B; Sample answer: To answer the first question, Yep says that his world was so unlike the world of Homer Price that those books were alien to him (lines 16–18). **2.** C; Sample answer: The word *prolific* is in a sentence that lists many different kinds of books that Yep has written. So, I picked C because I think *prolific* means very productive—60 books is a lot (lines 1–8). **3.** Sample answer: He liked how characters in those kinds of books had to adapt all the time to strange places, languages, and customs. He recalls felling that way every day (lines 18–21). **4.** Sample answer: In this passage, the ellipses let you know that something was left out of the original quotation. **5.** Sample answer: Yep means that he enjoyed writing so much that he kept at it from then on (lines 24–25).

6. Sample answer: I think Yep means that writers write about what they know best (line 27), even very ordinary or everyday things. Writers also put their own spin on experiences or observations based on their feelings and memories that others often want to forget (lines 33–35).

Passage 12: Ancient Survivor

1. D; Sample answer: The paragraph with that sentence opens with the word *Survivor* in boldface. Survivors probably aren't frail (line 10). **2.** B; Sample answer: I figured out that *flourish* means to survive well, and in line 23 it says that the gingko can withstand wide temperature swings. Cacti that live in very dry, hot places flourish, so I picked *desert* (lines 16–25). **3.** Sample answer: The ginkgo is an ancient survivor. It is over 270 million years old (lines 10–12), and it has survived harsh conditions (line 21–30) and destructive catastrophes (lines 1–9). **4.** Sample answer: I think that "tip your hat" means to show respect or admiration. The author wants us to respect how remarkable, amazing, and unique the ginkgo is (line 10). **5.** Sample answer: Allies work together to help each other. Humans help ginkgo trees by planting them all over the place and caring for them; ginkgo trees help humans by adding beauty and green to cities where other trees might fail (lines 16–30). **6.** Sample answer: I know that the prefix *bi-* means two, as in *bicycle*. So, I think that *biloba* is a scientific way to say that each ginkgo leaf has two parts, or two lobes. The photo shows this.

Passage 13: Lessons From Superheroes

1. A; Sample answer: I reread the first paragraph, about superheroes in comics and now in movies, plays, and TV. I see them everywhere, so *ever-present* seems like the best answer (lines 1–13). **2.** B; Sample answer: In lines 21 and 22, the author says that *altruistic* means doing good without expecting a reward. In choices A and D you get money, which is a reward, and writing a thank-you note is expected. Donating to a food drive seems altruistic. **3.** Sample answer: This essay grabs readers with a riddle-like question to think about. It makes us want to keep reading (lines 1–3). **4.** Sample answer: A *backstory* is like background information. It tells what happened to characters earlier in their lives that explains or affects how they are now. A writer might tell you this to surprise you or help you better understand the character (lines 29–36). **5.** Sample answer: The author's main conclusion is that super heroes teach us about coping with problems and about showing compassion and empathy. Those traits are far more important than having super powers like X-ray vision (lines 39–47). **6.** Answers will vary. Sample answer: A hero is someone you look up to, trust, can count on, and can learn from. Like the author says, a hero shows compassion and empathy, and tries to make the world a better place, even in small ways (lines 43–47).

Passage 14: Impossible Not to Smile

1. A; Sample answer: Geri Jewell said, "Questions don't hurt. Ignorance does." This tells me that she welcomes questions (lines 22–25). **2.** D; Sample answer: This expression asks the reader to think about why Geri does the things she does, so I picked D (lines 19–21). **3.** Sample answer: She believes in not letting fear get in the way of what a person wants to do or achieve in life (lines 34–35). **4.** Sample answer: First, she was born with a brain disorder and has dealt with it her whole life, so she knows firsthand about the issues people face (lines 5–11). She even started a disability awareness center (lines 16–19). A good speaker knows how to make people feel at ease and connect with an audience. She is honest and direct about her challenges, has a good sense of humor, and makes the subject less awkward for people (lines 12–15). **5.** Sample answer: Geri Jewell made jokes about cerebral palsy to make the topic less daunting (lines 13–15); she doesn't hide her disability (lines 3–4); and she is comfortable talking about disabilities in a straightforward way (lines 16–19). **6.** Sample answer: The bumblebee can fly though its wings seem too small to carry it. Geri Jewell believes that she can do whatever she sets her mind to, even if it seems unlikely (lines 10–11, 36–44).

Passage 15: Ellis Island of the West

1. B; Sample answer: A is true (line 37), C is true (lines 3–5), and D is true (line 5). But the essay doesn't say that the island had schools. **2.** A; Sample answer: The author writes that the men and women waited sadly and listlessly (lines 22–24), and that they were angry, afraid, and frustrated (lines 24–27). **3.** Sample answer: Ellis Island was the famous place on the east coast where immigrants arrived; Angel Island served the same purpose on the west coast (lines 1–5). **4.** Sample answer: Officials didn't want newcomers to take away jobs from American workers so they needed a reason to refuse entry. If they asked really hard or strange questions that the immigrants had to struggle to answer, they would have an excuse to send them back (lines 10–20). **5.** Sample answer: In the essay, the author explained about the interrogations (lines 17–20). The quote helps make the author's point because Mr. Gee tells his personal version of preparing for the terrible interrogations, how much time he spent trying to get ready, and how strange and difficult the questions might be (sidebar). **6.** Sample answer: People who *emigrate* leave a country for another; people who *immigrate* arrive at a new country.

Passage 16: Game of Change

1. B; Sample answer: I didn't read anything about the heights of players. Jerry Harkness was the Loyola captain (lines 31–32), and I know that the Maroons lost in Round 2 (lines 29–30). The essay also says that all of the Maroons were white (lines 14–16). **2.** A; Sample answer: It says in lines 5–7 that the winning team of a single-elimination tournament was the national champion. That meant one loss knocked the other team out of the rest of the tournament. So, the champions did not lose at all (lines 12–14, 29–30). **3.** Sample answer: Some members of the Mississippi State team and fans felt prejudiced toward blacks, and did not want to compete against an integrated team (lines 20–24). **4.** Sample answer: Along with explaining the NCAA tournament and how exciting an event it was, the author grabs the reader's interest by suggesting that something very important will take place beyond determining a champion (lines 6–9). **5.** Sample answer: He must have opposed segregation because he stood up to the governor of the state to help his team get to the tournament. So, I think he was brave and wanted to do the right thing (lines 26–27). **6.** Sample answer: The title is the nickname of that historic NCAA game (lines 35–37). The change was that, for the first time, an all-white team from the South competed against an integrated team (lines 10–16). This match-up probably put an end to segregation on college basketball teams (lines 17–27).

Passage 17: Preserving Audio Archives

1. D; Sample answer: Of the choices, only a piece of sheet music cannot record and make sound (lines 9–12, 20–21). **2.** C; Sample answer: I know that software gets outdated and replaced by newer, better versions. So, I read each choice and asked myself which one is no longer in use (lines 25–28). **3.** Sample answer: A curator must make choices about what to add to a collection. The curators of the audio archives try to choose works that are important to the history of America (lines 9–20). **4.** Sample answer: I think the speech is given to a variety of young people with many interests, so it might be a class, a tour group, a club, or a group of visitors to Washington, D.C. (lines 1–3, 38–39). **5.** Sample answer: The speaker believes that the recordings are a national treasure because they are invaluable and important since they reveal a lot about American culture, history, innovation, and ideas (lines 6–7, 9–14, 16–21, 28–35). **6.** Sample answer: The recordings hold so much valuable and impossible-to-replace sound information that they must be kept in the best possible condition so they will last for years to come (lines 13–14, 22–35).

Passage 18: The Sky's the Limit

1. C; Sample answer: I learned from the essay that two innovations occurred at about the same time (lines 6–9). **2.** D; Sample answer: I read that the building was unique because steel frames supported its walls (lines 13–14). **3.** Sample answer: They were all involved in manufacturing or improving elevators (lines 19–26). **4.** Sample answer: I know that a city's skyline is how the shape of its buildings look from far away. So, I think the author means that the many new buildings in Chicago changed how it looked (lines 29–33). **5.** Sample answer: Chicago needed to be rebuilt, and people were coming up with new ideas for architecture. So, it would be a chance for architects to try some of their new ideas (lines 14–17, 26–28, 29–33). **6.** Sample answer: An accidental fire destroyed a large section of Chicago (lines 4–6). At the same time, there were important new developments in architecture that allowed buildings to be made taller, sturdier, and fireproof

(lines 11–17). The speed and safety of elevators also improved, allowing buildings to become much taller (lines 22–28). So, architects went to Chicago to rebuild it better and safer than before with those new techniques (lines 29–36).

Passage 19: Not Rocket Science

1. B; Sample answer: The author writes that true rockets operate solely by combustion and self-propulsion (line 13). **2.** C; Sample answer: I read all the choices in place of *Ingenuity* in that sentence. The one that fits best is *Inventiveness*, which is about experiments and trying things (lines 2–3, 7–8, 24–26). **3.** Sample answer: They were trying to find ways to make people live forever. But instead, the materials they mixed combusted and made things move, like a rocket (lines 19–30). **4.** Sample answer: I know that a mortal doesn't live forever, and *im-* is a prefix that means *not*, so immortality means not dying. The essay gives a synonym a few lines later: *everlasting life* (line 23). **5.** Sample answer: I think maybe these are the closest words we have in English to the Chinese descriptions of those two things. Also, these words probably describe how these early rockets looked and acted (lines 13–17, 26–32). **6.** Sample answer: This essay explains that the discovery of rocketry did not happen because people were trying to invent rockets. It came about by accident (lines 5–6, 19–24, 33–36).

Passage 20: Surprises in Ice

1. D; Sample answer: In lines 16 and 17, it says that scientists wanted to find out if there was a relationship between warm climates and increased methane gas levels. So, *implicated* must be close in meaning to A, B, and C. Only *cleared* changes the meaning of *implicated* in the first sentence. **2.** C; Sample answer: The graph shows methane gas at 9%, which is about one-tenth. **3.** Sample answer: They found that methane levels did change over time, but not in step with changes in temperature, as they'd once thought (lines 18–21). **4.** Sample answer: Scientists now think that the changes are linked to changes in population, agriculture, and manufacturing—even before the Industrial Revolution (lines 23–27). **5.** Sample answer: I think that those centuries must have been when the Industrial Revolution took place, because that's when scientists used to think methane gas first rose (lines 7–9, 35–39). **6.** Sample answer: I might want to know: How does this amount compare with the amounts produced by other countries, or by the United States at other times in history? (lines 1–6, 35–39).

Passage 21: Astronomers' Desert

1. D; Sample answer: I think that *arid* means dry, because the Atacama is one of the driest places in the world. So, visitors there better be sure to have drinking water (lines 2–5, 9–11). **2.** A; Sample answer: With so little water in the Atacama, you wouldn't find B, C, or D. The article does mention mining camps, so I picked A (lines 2–5, 13–14). **3.** Sample answer: It sits at a high altitude, has dry, thin air, almost no cloud cover, and little light pollution. These make it a great place for telescopes (lines 15–18). **4.** Sample answer: I know that glaciers are masses of ice, which must need water to form. So, even though the mountains are high enough for water to freeze, not enough of it falls from the sky (lines 4–5, 9–11). **5.** Sample answer: It's the world's largest radio telescope, and astronomers using it can see things incredibly far away that they've never seen before; they see nearer things more clearly than ever (lines 21–31). **6.** Sample answer: Astronomers observe the sky through telescopes. So, the places they choose for their observation labs are very dependent on good locations. According to the article, dry and high desert conditions on Earth are best for clear observation (lines 1–18).

Passage 22: The Great Wall of Los Angeles

1. B; Sample answer: The article clearly states that Baca is an artist, educator, activist, and community arts pioneer. I picked B because it most closely matches that description (lines 5–6). **2.** C; Sample answer: In the opening quote, Baca says that she wants to give voice to people who may not be represented in any visual way (lines 2–4). She is interested in working to build interracial harmony (line 11). **3.** Sample answer: I see that *insurmountable* describes obstacles, which are things that block you. I see the root *mount,* which means to climb. The prefix *in-* means not, *sur* means on or over, and the suffix *able* means can do it. Put altogether, *insurmountable* means not able to be climbed over. A synonym for this word is *impossible.* **4.** Sample answer: I know that landmarks are buildings or features with some kind of importance. So, I think that cultural landmarks are works of creativity that reflect things of value to a culture. The wall depicts the culture of Los Angeles over time (lines 8–11, 17–23). **5.** Sample answer: Since kids and families worked on it together, they did most of the work in summers (lines 13–15). They painted it panel by panel (line 16) and it is a half-mile long (line 8). **6.** Sample answer: I can see how very high it is because people need to use ladders to work on it. I also see by the truck that it's even bigger than I thought at first, and I notice more than one person working on it.

Passage 23: Bad Burger

1. B; Sample answer: In the opening paragraph, the writer raves about the things she likes about Best Burgers, so I picked B (lines 6–11). There is no mention at all of price, portions, or location or going there because of new equipment. **2.** A; Sample answer: In the second paragraph I read that unpalatable foods aren't good to eat (lines 15–20), so I chose A. **3.** Sample answer: I think it means that she can't decide. It says in line 28 that Julia is not sure if she should return to what was once her favorite restaurant after such a disappointing meal (lines 25–29). **4.** Sample answer: She made a point of bringing out-of-town friends to a place she expected would impress them (lines 11–13), but the terrible meal made her feel awful and embarrassed. **5.** Sample answer: The letter begins with a list of compliments about the restaurant to show that the writer

appreciates the restaurant (lines 6–11). Only after that does the writer announce her disappointment (lines 11–13). This approach might grab the manager's attention more than a list of complaints. **6.** Sample answer: I think the letter is friendly, respectful, clear, detailed, informative, even understanding, though the writer has been disappointed.

Passage 24: Off-Leash

1. B; Sample answer: The writer does A (lines 2–24), C (lines 62–72), and D (lines 25–51), but she doesn't sound angry. **2.** D; Sample answer: The writer describes the roads in the parks as being clogged with runners, walkers, and cyclists, so this sounds like it's crowded (lines 32–36). **3.** Sample answer: The writer talks about dogs being able to run free without hindrance. So, I think a hindrance is something that holds the dog back or limits the dog's freedom, such as a leash (lines 18–24, 36–40). **4.** Sample answer: I think that she used *whirring* because that word is like the sound a bunch of cyclists make as they speed by. **5.** Sample answer: Rosen's tone is polite, friendly, and calm. She shows concern for her community and neighbors, and is reasonable and helpful in her suggested solution (lines 10–14, 36–40, 52–65, 77–81). **6.** Sample answer: I think the writer sees her issue as a community problem that affects anyone who shares the city parks. If the letter appears in the newspaper, her issue will get more attention.

Passage 25: Table Tennis

1. D; Sample answer: The descriptions of the racquet name its parts. The hitting surface is the blade (lines 18–20). **2.** C; Sample answer: I reread the paragraph about the table. I found its length (2.74 m) and width (1.52 m) and estimated their product (line 5). **3.** Sample answer: I think it's so players can easily see the white lines on the table and the ball, which is white or orange (line 21). **4.** Sample answer: No. The rules state that a game isn't over until the winner has 2 points more than the opponent (lines 23–29). **5.** Sample answer: The audience might include gym teachers, people learning to play table tennis, people who plan to buy a table and equipment for this game, game judges, and sports writers. **6.** Answers will vary. Sample answer: I don't know how a game begins, who serves first, where players may stand, if there is an official, what you have to wear (or not), how big the paddle blade can be, how long a game can last, or if there are penalties or out-of-bounds rules.

25 Complex Text Passages to Meet the Common Core: Literature and Informational Texts, Grade 6 © 2014 by Scholastic Teaching Resources